Taking the Plunge

A Teen's Guide to Independence

Laura Purdie Salas
CHILD & FAMILY PRESS
WASHINGTON, DC

Child & Family Press is an imprint of the Child Welfare League of America. The Child Welfare League of America is the nation's oldest and largest membership-based child welfare organization. We are committed to engaging people everywhere in promoting the well-being of children, youth, and their families, and protecting every child from harm. All proceeds from the sale of this book support CWLA's programs in behalf of children and families.

CHILD WELFARE LEAGUE OF AMERICA, INC.
HEADQUARTERS
440 First Street, NW, Third Floor, Washington, DC 20001-2085
E-mail: books@cwla.org

CURRENT PRINTING (last digit)
10 9 8 7 6 5 4 3 2 1

Cover and text design by Michael Rae
Edited by Julie Gwin

Printed in the United States of America

ISBN # 1-58760-012-9

Library of Congress Cataloging-in-Publication Data

Salas, Laura Purdie.
  Taking the plunge : a teen's guide to independence / Laura Purdie Salas.
    p. cm.
  Includes bibliographical references (p.   ).
  ISBN 1-58760-012-9 (alk. paper)
    1. Teenagers--Life skills guides--Juvenile literature. 2. Teenagers--Conduct of life--Juvenile literature. 3. Autonomy in adolescence--Juvenile literature. I. Title.
HQ796.S242 2003
646.7'0084'2--dc22   2003025373

Dedication

To Gail, Patty, and J.P. Thanks for being my support team and my sisters.
And to Randy, thanks for being you.

Contents

CHAPTER 1

Take a Deep Breath
Before You Dive into Independence

Imagine you are at the pool, and you want to try a new skill on the high dive. Your friends watch while you climb the ladder. You take a deep breath, think about the dive, and start your approach. A moment later, you are hurtling toward the water at high speed. If you make a spectacular dive, your friends cheer and give you high-fives. If you land in a painful belly flop, they help you out of the water and encourage you to try again.

Becoming independent is like going off the high dive. You have to plan it if you want to do a good job. It's scary, but exciting. You will need plenty of friends, a support team, to encourage you whether you score a perfect 10 or crash and burn.

So, you are probably thinking about becoming independent. Maybe you are moving away to college. Or you might be part of a family with no home. Maybe you can't stand living with your parents, or maybe they are kicking you out. You might not even have a family.

It is very important to make plans. If you just run away, with no clear-cut plans, you could end up living on the streets. Kids on the streets beg or do things they don't want to do to get money for food. They might be physically abused, raped, or beaten because they don't have a safe place to be. They go to bed hungry, or cold, or in pain. Most of all, they really don't have control over their lives. But if you make plans, you can build a life for yourself. A life where you work hard, have fun, hang out with your friends, and control your own future.

Around 300,000 teens live on the streets in the United States.

How Old Is Old Enough?

The hard truth is that very few kids younger than 16 can build a truly independent life. Laws about school, work, and driving all make it hard for a 15-year-old to live independently.

If you are 15 or younger, please talk to someone about your problems. When I was 13, I knew I couldn't wait to move out of my parents' house. But I also knew I would have nowhere to sleep, no way to eat, and no way to get around. So I stuck it out and moved out when I was 16. If you can't stick it out, if your home life is completely unbearable, please check out the bibliography at the end of the book and call a hotline or one of the agencies listed and tell someone what is going on in your life. No matter what you think, the people there will not be shocked by what you tell them. They can try to help you.

If you are at least 16, then you are old enough to do amazing things for yourself, no matter what other people tell you.

Independent Life—An independent life is one in which you control your own actions and take care of yourself. Although you may not legally be an adult, if you live an independent life, you will have most of the same privileges and responsibilities that adults do.

Quiz

Am I Ready for Independence?

For each question, circle the answer that best describes you. Use the key at the end to add up your points.

1. **Do I turn my homework in on time?**
   a. No, I turn it in early.
   b. Well, I would, but I usually get busy with other things. Besides, they assign too much homework.
   c. Yes, I'm a good student and I finish my assignments on time.
   d. I finish it, but I usually can't find it to turn it in.
   e. Most of the time my homework is too hard.

2. **Can I take orders?**
   a. Definitely.
   b. It depends if I agree with the order or not.
   c. No. People shouldn't be ordering me around. I'm practically an adult.
   d. I follow orders if they are from my parents, my teachers, or my boss.
   e. I would, but I often don't understand what they want me to do.

3. **Do I have a way to make money?**
   a. I don't need money. My friends said I could stay with them.
   b. I have a job, but I don't think I could live off the amount I make.
   c. Yes, but I hate it or it's illegal.
   d. I have a pretty good job, and I've been saving up for the last two years.
   e. No, my last boss fired me just because she didn't like me.

4. **Am I willing to work really hard?**
   a. No! If I wanted to work really hard, I would just stay at home. My parents make me do way too much stuff.
   b. Yes. I know it'll be tough, but I will do whatever I need to to be independent.
   c. No, but it won't be that hard.
   d. I'll try, but my teachers and bosses tell me I'm too slow or I'm not trying hard enough.
   e. Yes. I love to work hard, and I like challenges.

5. **Am I determined to be independent?**
   a. Not really. I just thought it sounded like fun. Less hassles.
   b. Yes. I can't stand it at home anymore. I have to live on my own.
   c. Yes, and I always accomplish what I set out to do.
   d. I don't know. My boyfriend/girlfriend thinks I would be better off living on my own.
   e. I don't know. I'd like to try it.

6. **Do I have a way to get to my job, school, the doctor, and so forth?**
   a. I have a moped that I use to get around.
   b. No, but my parents and my friends will take me places.
   c. No, because I got two tickets, and my parents took away my car.
   d. I'm planning to buy a really cool new car as soon as I graduate.
   e. I have some money saved up, but I'm waiting to see where I will work. Meanwhile, I ride the bus everywhere I need to go.

7. **Do I have a support system made up of people who can help me in an emergency or with my everyday questions?**
   a. I'm building one. I've been talking to my guidance counselor, my two older sisters, and the financial aid person at the college I want to attend. I have two good friends who will help me when I need help.
   b. I don't need help. That's the whole point of independence.
   c. I'm sure my friends will do whatever I ask them to.
   d. Yes, I have spoken with many people (guidance counselor, boss, 18 friends, and my grandmother, for starters, plus a doctor, a mechanic, and the towing company). I already have all their numbers on speed dial on my cell phone.
   e. No, I don't really know who to ask for help.

Scoring

1. Independent people finish things on time. When a bill, or tax form, or a work project is due, adults are expected to have them finished on time.

        a = 5   b = 1   c = 4   d = 2   e = 3

2. Maybe you thought being independent meant nobody told you what to do. Think again. Everyone takes orders from someone. You will still have to follow directions from bosses, teachers, police officers, landlords, and other people in authority.

        a = 5   b = 2   c = 1   d = 4   e = 3

3. Apartments, food, clothes, transportation...they all cost money. In 1999, kids between 16 and 19 years old earned an average of $6.08 per hour. Even if you work 40 hours per week, you'll earn only $243.20 per week and $972.80 per month. If you are very careful with your money, you can live on that amount, but you will probably be sharing a low-rent apartment with roommates and driving an old car or taking the bus. And you would be working all day, five days a week, just to get by. That is not too scary if you plan to continue your schooling or job training. A few years at a fast-food restaurant or sales job will not be too bad. But if you have no plans to improve your job skills, you might end up with no plans for the future except for flipping burgers or bagging groceries.

        a = 2   b = 4   c = 3   d = 5   e = 1

4. Being responsible for yourself is hard work. Maybe you think your parents nag you too much. But will you be able to take care of yourself without their nagging? Can you get yourself up on time for work or school? Can you go grocery shopping and cook? Do your own laundry? Manage your own bank account?

        a = 1   b = 4   c = 2   d = 3   e = 5

5. If you are unsure about moving out and think you'll just give it a try, you will probably end up back home, and things might be worse then than they are now. If you are truly determined to make it work, then you will plan and work hard to ensure that you do not fail.

        a = 2   b = 4   c = 5   d = 1   e = 3

6. You have to be able to go places to be independent. If you live in a big city, the subway, bus, or train system might be all you need. If you live in a college town or a very small town, your own two feet, a bicycle, or inline skates can get you around. But if you live in the suburbs or in a rural area, where there is no transit system and stores and offices are pretty spread out, you will need a car, or maybe a moped.

        a = 4   b = 2   c = 1   d = 3   e = 5

7. Independence means taking care of yourself, but that does not mean you won't need help. You will need a support system, which is just a fancy name for people who can help you. Perhaps you have a friend with a car who is willing to take you to the doctor when you are sick. Maybe your school guidance counselor is helping you apply for financial aid for college. Maybe your roommate is there to encourage you when you are feeling rotten. These people are your support system.

  a = 4   b = 2   c = 1   d = 5   e = 3

What Your Score Tells You

0–7 Too dependent!

You are depending on other people too much. True independence does not mean bunking with friends and depending on them to take you everywhere. It does not mean blaming your boss if you get fired or blaming your teachers for giving you homework. You are not ready to be independent until you can accept responsibility for what you do and what you don't do. Once you get into the habit of more responsible actions, you will be better suited for independence.

8–14 Not determined enough

If you want to live on your own, you are going to need to be more realistic and more determined. Use this book to find out what you need to do to be independent. You probably need to develop some of the same habits that annoy you in other people—being more responsible, turning things in on time, showing up to work and school on time, following a schedule, thinking about the consequences of your actions, or sticking with a job you dislike because you know you have bills to pay. If this all sounds horrible to you, accept the fact that independence is a huge job that you don't want to take on. There's nothing wrong with that, and it is better to discover it now than later.

15–21 Short on skills

If you're having problems at school and at your job, it's likely you are going to run into problems with independence. If you feel you have to be independent, be sure to assemble a large support team. Find an adult you like and trust to give you some guidance. Independence will be tough, but if you are really determined and are willing to work hard, you can do it.

22–28 Up to the task

You have the skills and habits you need to be successfully independent. If you feel ready to move out, you probably are. Continue to organize your support team and make plans for your successful, independent life.

29–35 Independent and in charge!

You're so organized and logical, you could be running your own company, maybe even your own small country! Well, at least you are well prepared to run your own life.

What Laws Affect Your Independence?

Labor Laws

There are laws about how many hours kids can work. The government put these laws into place to protect children and to allow them time to grow up and go to school. Different states have different laws, but most states say that kids younger than 14 cannot work. Kids who are 14 and 15 can only work three hours per day, with a maximum of 18 hours per week. Obviously, you cannot earn enough money to live off of if you can only work 18 hours per week.

Proficiency Exam—A test to prove that you have the minimum skills to be allowed to withdraw from school. Once you pass the exam, you will earn your GED, or General Education Development certificate. A GED will allow you more job and education opportunities than if you just drop out of school. More than 500,000 Americans earned GEDs in 1998. Some people with GEDs go on to successful careers, like comedian Bill Cosby, gymnast Mary Lou Retton, Wendy's founder Dave Thomas, and U.S. Senator Ben Nighthorse Campbell.

Kids who are 16 and older generally have fewer restrictions. Call your state's department of labor to find out what the child labor laws are in your state. Check out http://www.dol.gov/esa/contacts/state_of.htm to find the name, phone number, and website of your state's labor department.

School Laws

Different states have different ages at which children can stop going to school. In many states, kids must attend school until they are at least 16. Even to quit school at 16, you frequently need your parents' permission. Some states require that you attend school until you are 18 or until you pass a proficiency exam. Talk to the guidance counselor at your school to find out what laws apply to you. If that is not an option, check with your state's education department. Check Appendix B for contact information.

Driving Laws

This is another set of laws that can help or hurt your chance of independence. If you move out of the house at the age of 13, you cannot drive for another few years. Most states allow you to get a junior license or a learner's permit at 15 and a license at 16, but only if you have taken a driver's education class and passed the license examination. In some states, you must be older than 16 to get a license. Be sure to call your state's department of motor vehicles (see Appendix A) and check on the requirements in your state. Many states allow you to drive a moped at the age of 15, after you pass driving tests.

Learner's Permit—A learner's permit is a driver's license that allows you to drive only under certain conditions. Those conditions vary from state to state. Some common restrictions include driving only with a fully licensed driver, driving only during daylight hours, and staying off certain highways.

Overwhelmed?

Maybe you are thinking that independence sounds like a whole lot of work. You're right. Adults' lives are full of rules and responsibilities. Your mom and dad might cut you some slack if you don't get the garbage out on time, and your teacher might give you an extra day or two for an assignment if you are sick. But when you are living independently, you will discover that your boss likely won't pay you for time that you are out sick, and the power company will cut off your electricity if you are late with a bill. When you are independent, blowing off your responsibilities has bigger consequences.

By the Numbers   **Age Minimums**

To earn a regular driver's license . . . . .16–18, varies by state

To quit school . . . . .16–18, varies by state

To sign a lease 18*

To work part-time . . . . .Generally 14

To work full-time . . . . .Generally 16, varies by state

To get a car loan 18*

* In some states, a minor (a person younger than 18) can sign a contract only if an adult signs it also, or cosigns. That adult agrees to be responsible for the payments or other terms of the contract if the minor does not follow the contract. Generally, both the adult and the minor will have to be approved by the bank or landlord.

So, what can you do? Well, if you are unhappy at home but think independence would be too hard for you, you have a couple of options. First, you might decide that your best bet is to stick it out at home for a few more years. A few years can sound like forever, I know. But use that time to get prepared for independence. Get a part-time job. Save up money. Think about what kind of job or career you would like to pursue, and find out how much school or training it requires. If you are 13 or 14 years old, even just making it at home until you're 16 will make independence easier. If you are already 16, try sticking it out until you finish high school.

Maybe staying at home a few more years doesn't work for you. There is an alternative. Try a semi-independent lifestyle. This usually hinges on a job that includes food and shelter. Military, nanny, camp counselor—all of these jobs and many more allow you to work at a job, earn money, and make your own decisions, but they all also include housing and meals! That takes care of two of your major concerns. Many semi-independent jobs are positions of great responsibility. When shelter is provided as part of a job, you are expected to take good care of it, so this lifestyle is a compromise. You don't get much choice about your housing and possibly your food, but you don't have to hunt for an apartment, grocery shop, cook, pay utility bills, or find transportation to work. This can be a terrific way to ease into independence and gain job experience.

Staying with a friend or family member for six months to a year is another way to live semi-independently. Perhaps the family of a good friend or your older brother or sister will let you stay with them while you get your life in order. You can save up money for a car, continue going to school, and otherwise prepare for independence. Just remember that the person you are staying with will expect certain things from you. Helping out around the house, staying in school, and keeping your room clean are a few likely possibilities. Be sure to talk with them about exactly what they expect before you make the decision.

A fourth option exists if you absolutely cannot stay at home and even semi-independence sounds too tough to tackle. You might hate to hear it, but you really need to turn to an adult. If you can't live on your own and you can't stay at home, you need help from a number of people. If you are in an abusive situation, tell a teacher, a guidance counselor, or a crisis hotline. If your parents are kicking you out of the house and you are younger than 18, tell someone. If you're afraid for your safety, please, please tell someone. Living with foster parents may sound terrible. Confronting your parents may sound unbearable. But you have to be strong, strong enough to admit you can't do it on your own. If you don't have anybody you can tell, check out Chapter 3, "Teamwork: Finding the People Who Will Support You." Call one of the national hotlines listed at the end of the chapter. Most of them can talk to you about your options and refer you to local organizations that can help you.

Options for Semi-independence

The Military

You must be at least 17 years old to join the armed forces. If you are just 17, your parents must sign a permission slip. Most, but not all, programs require a high school diploma. The military also offers scholarships, where you go to college and then serve in the military, or you attend school and also serve in the reserve program or the National Guard while still in college. As a member of the military, you receive free food, free housing, and free medical and dental care. You also will get training in a good career. Check out http://www.armedforcescareers.com for information.

The Peace Corps

You have to be 18 to join the Peace Corps, and most assignments require related work experience or a college degree. This will likely be an option for you only if you have some specific skills that the Peace Corps needs. Assignments are for two years and three months, so this is not a short-term option. For more information, see http://www.peacecorps.gov/indexf.cfm.

Missionary Work

Obviously, this is not something you do just to get free room and board. But if you feel a strong spiritual calling, you can talk to your minister about the possibility of missionary work. Be very honest about what you are looking for and your limited resources. Your minister may know about some situations that would be just right for you.

Camp Counselor

Most camps hire counselors from their pool of counselors-in-training, but you might have a luck finding a job on the kitchen crew or maintenance crew. The pay will not be fantastic, but if you like outdoor settings, a summer camp job will give you a chance to save up some money and get room and board.

House Sitter

This is another job where you'll have more luck finding a position if you are older than 18. People only trust their homes to others they see as very responsible. Try starting out with people you know. Do a great job for them, and then ask them to write you a letter of reference. Letters of reference from your teachers or guidance counselors praising your trustworthiness can also help you find a gig.

Nanny/Au Pair

This is a person who lives with a family while providing child care and light housework. Many au pair (oh-PARE) organizations have a minimum age of 18. Generally, you must have a high school diploma. You can look for a position in the United States or in another country. Au pairs receive room and board plus some spending money.

Contact an au pair organization or check your local classified ads for live-in nannies. You might work 30 or more hours a week for room and board plus about $100 per week. Some organizations charge you a fee to match you up with a family; others charge the fee to the family. Most positions ask for a one-year commitment. Visit http://www.iapa.org/.

Caretaker/Apartment Manager

To get this position, you have to be handy with tools and good with people. You have to be organized and responsible, as well. A caretaker or apartment manager job usually includes a rent-free apartment or living space.

TOP 10

Ten Semi-independent Living Situations

1. Staying with an older sibling
2. Moving in with a friend who is still living at home
3. Armed forces
4. Camp counselor (generally summer only)
5. House sitter
6. Live-in babysitter
7. Live-in housekeeper
8. Apartment manager
9. Live-in maid, waiter, gardener (at an inn or for an individual)
10. Worker at tourist attraction that provides employee housing

Service Jobs

Sometimes hotels, inns, and wealthy people hire staff to live on the premises. Some likely jobs include maid, waiter, gardener, and stable worker. Look for independently owned hotels or inns. Chains like Marriott and Holiday Inn do not generally have employees living on site. A small bed and breakfast isn't going to offer room and board either, because it won't have the extra space. But a large inn or hotel run by a single owner might offer room and board plus lower wages, because they have the space. You need the mid-size establishments to have a shot. You won't find these advertised online, for the most part. Get a list of lodging possibilities in your area, then write a great resume and cover letter and send one off to every establishment on the list.

Tourist Worker

Where have you always dreamed of going? National parks, amusement parks, resorts, dude ranches? Maybe you can work there. Many of these locations hire live-in staff for the summers. In the newspaper and online, you will see the higher-scale jobs listed, the ones that require experience or training. But some of the bigger and more isolated resorts offer room and board to all their staff, including kitchen workers, maintenance workers, and others. Find attractions that offer room and board for at least some of their employees, and then e-mail, call, or write to them and see if they have other live-in positions available.

Many of these semi-independent positions are a huge responsibility, and some of them will take you far from home. If your parents are not guiding you, find an adult you trust to help you understand exactly what your responsibilities and costs will be with any of these programs.

See Chapter 5, "Going Pro: Choosing the Right Job or Career," for job-hunting tips, including how to write a resume and a cover letter, how to find places to apply, and how to use the Internet to help with your job search.

CHAPTER 2

Climbing the Ladder
Reaching Your Goals Rung by Rung

A lot of people have probably talked to you about setting goals. You may have ignored all that advice, because reaching goals always seems to involve a lot of hard work.

Well, sit back and listen up, because you really do need goals.

Setting goals is simply defining what you want. That's not so hard, is it? Maybe your biggest goal right now is moving out of the house. If so, there you go. You've set a goal. Maybe you have other goals, too: I want to be a nurse. I want to own my own house. I want to go to college. I want a fun job. I want time to spend with my friends. I want to be in charge of my own life.

By knowing what your goals are, you make it easier to make choices that will help you reach them. A practical goal is a concrete thing that can be measured. So, if you say, "I want to be in charge of my own life," that's a hard thing to measure. But if you say, "I want to live in my own apartment in six months and pay my own rent," that's something that you can look at in six months and say, "Yes, I accomplished that," or "No, I didn't."

How to Set Goals

I am a big believer in both goals and dreams, but I don't necessarily think they are the same thing. I might dream of living on a Caribbean island and teaching windsurfing all day. But is that my goal? No. I know it's not because I have never tried to pursue it, I can think of all sorts of reasons I really *don't* want to do it, and I don't even know how to windsurf. I just like to fantasize about that life sometimes when I'm tired, it's grey and snowy, and I have to get up and go to work.

If living on a Caribbean island and teaching windsurfing all day really was my goal, I would be actively working toward it, trying to make it a reality. That's what I do with goals.

First, I make sure my big goal is something I really want to do, stated in a positive way. In other words, don't say, "I don't want to live with my parents." Instead, state it positively: I want to live on my own, as a responsible adult.

Next, I break my goal into concrete mini-goals. If I were trying to make that Caribbean dream come true, my mini-goals might include: Learn to windsurf, research Caribbean islands, find out how expensive it is to live in the Caribbean, research owning a small business in the Caribbean, and so on.

I might even break each mini-goal into small steps. I would break "learn to windsurf" into the following steps:

1. Check the Yellow Pages for windsurfing stores.

2. Call the county park system for information.

3. Call windsurfing equipment stores to find out about lessons.

4. Start saving up $25 per week until I have enough for a beginner's course.

5. Look for inexpensive equipment rental places.

6. Find out if I can work an hour or two each day in exchange for an hour's worth of equipment rental.

7. Practice four days a week.

8. Look for inexpensive used windsurfing equipment.

By breaking down a big goal into mini-goals, and then breaking those mini-goals down into steps, I keep from being overwhelmed. Can I move to the Caribbean tomorrow and teach windsurfing? No. But if I really want to, I now know some of the steps to follow to make that goal a reality.

Make sure those mini-goals and steps are concrete and measurable. Then you will have a real sense of accomplishment at meeting each goal. If your goal is to improve your social life, that's fine. But when you set mini-goals, be more specific. Maybe mini-goals that would make you happier with your social life include: I will get together with friends one night per week; I will go out on one date per week (blind or otherwise); and within two months, I will join a group or class where I'll meet people my age with similar interests. Each one of those mini-goals is measurable. You will know when you have accomplished it. See Worksheet 1 on page 15 to start setting some basic short-term and long-term goals.

I also like to set deadlines. A long-term goal of, say, owning a house, might have a deadline five years away. A shorter-term deadline, like improving your social life, might

Running Away Versus Moving Out

- Running away is when you leave home with no means to support yourself and no way to truly live independently. When you run away, you have no plan, and you usually end up with no control over your life.

- Moving out is making a choice to work hard and support yourself. It is being realistic, accepting responsibility, and making plans for an independent life. Moving out is a process of moving toward the life you want, not just away from the life you don't want.

How to Tell Your Parents

If you are reading this book, one of your goals is probably to move out on your own. That means you are going to have to tell your parents. Here are some tips for the best way to do it:

- Don't spit it out during an argument. Say, "I need to talk to you about something important. Can we talk tonight?" If you think your parents will be calm, helpful, and perhaps even supportive, give them enough time to get used to the idea, perhaps a few months before you plan to move out.

- Try not to accuse your parents of being mean, impossible to live with, or never satisfied. That might all be true, but saying it won't help the situation. Even if you plan on supporting yourself entirely, their cooperation will make some things easier for you. For instance, you might need information they have for financial aid forms.

- Simply say that you think it will be the best situation for everyone if you move out to live on your own.

- Ask straight out, politely, "Are you willing to help me?" If they are willing to keep you on their insurance policy, officially give you the car they bought for you to drive, and so forth, be appropriately grateful.

- Ask for your birth certificate, your social security card, your childhood medical records, and any other official paperwork you think you might need.

- Ask if they are willing to not claim you as a dependent on their tax return starting that year. That may make it easier for you to get assistance from various agencies.

- Outline your plans. Show them that you have given this a lot of thought, unless, of course, your parents are abusive and you are scared of them. In that case, I wouldn't share my plans with them.

- Make sure you mean it. Don't scream, "I'm moving out tomorrow" on the spur if the moment during a fight with your folks. They might start helping you pack.

be only two months away. If you know when you would like to accomplish your goal, it helps you to set deadlines for your mini-goals. Just work backward. If you want to move out of your parents' house in two years, then maybe you have mini-goals of buying a car in 18 months, discussing living and school options with your guidance counselor in one year, and getting a job to save up for a car and your general savings account right now.

Now you try. Make a copy of Worksheet 2 on page 16 and pick a goal to work on.

Mini-goals and Steps Too Complicated for You?

What if all this sounds like just too much work? Maybe goals, mini-goals, steps, and deadlines just don't do it for you. If the goalmaking process overwhelms you, try this one-step plan.

Just concentrate on your one stated goal. Perhaps it's buying a car. Then, each time you need to make a choice, you ask yourself, Will this take me closer to my goal or farther away from my goal?

When Your Parents Are Angry

Your parents could have many reactions to your independence. They might be sad, disappointed, amazed, indifferent, or angry. If your parents are enraged by your decision, the best thing to do is to stay away and give them some time to get used to your new life.

Sometimes, you still need their help (such as if you are semi-independent) or you just want to repair your relationship with them. Here are some practical tips for easing into or maintaining a relationship:

- Call when you know nobody's home and leave a "Just called to say hi" message.

- Send brief letters or cards letting them know how you are doing.

- Behave in an adult manner. Your parents should be proud of you, and if they're not, you should at least be proud of yourself!

- Don't take the bait. When Mom or Dad says something that always leads to the same old argument, try saying, "I guess we'll just have to agree to disagree."

- Avoid blame. Don't get caught up in discussions of why you moved out. To move beyond what they see as your betrayal or stupidity, ask them about their interests: their gardens, pets, jobs, whatever. Try to stick with less-controversial subjects until they get used to the idea of your being out on your own.

- If they are angry in a way that scares you, or if they have abused you in the past, don't have any contact with them by yourself. Any contact should be made only through a trusted adult, like a guidance counselor or a caseworker.

Rethinking the "F" Word

Think failure is bad? Think because you haven't reached your goal that you'll never make it? Think that because someone tells you, you can't, that you never will?

Think again.

Babe Ruth spent his childhood years in an orphanage and then struck out 1,330 times on his way to 714 home runs and baseball immortality.

Think of your obstacles as practice.

In 1954, Elvis Presley was fired from the Grand Ole Opry after only one performance, and the manager told him, "You ain't goin' nowhere, son. Better get y'all job back drivin' a truck."

Think of your adversities as rehearsals.

It took Thomas Edison years of performing experiments that didn't succeed before he invented the light bulb.

Think of your failures as research.

My point? Failure has gotten a bad rap. We are all responsible for this, and in doing so, we waste one of mankind's greatest resources...failure. It's our fear of using that resource that's killing so many possibilities! We must make failure a stepping stone to success. How? By learning, constantly reevaluating, not worrying about being perfect, ignoring others' judgments, and never, never giving up on your dreams!

Remember, the only real failure in failure is if it stops you from risking another failure.

—Steve Young, award-winning television writer, speaker, and author of *Great Failures of the Extremely Successful* (Tallfellow Press, 2002)

Worksheet 1

One-Year and Five-Year Goal Sheet

	NOW	ONE YEAR FROM NOW	FIVE YEARS FROM NOW
Home			
School			
Job			
Transportation			
Hobby or Interest			

Say you wake up and don't really feel like going to work. You are trying to decide whether to call in sick, so you ask yourself, "Will this take me closer to getting a car or farther away from getting a car?" Obviously, if you call in sick, you probably won't get paid. That means less money to save toward your car. Calling in sick, therefore, takes you farther away from your goal.

As often as possible, try to choose the option that will move you closer to your goal.

This easy, low-effort approach to goal-setting and -achieving works best with relatively short-term goals. It can be harder to see the connection if a goal is a long way in the future. It's hard to remember, for example, that you need to work that day to save more money, you need to save more money to buy the car, you need to buy the car to get to a community college 18 miles away next year, and you need to go to community college to get your hair-styling license. When you wake up feeling blah, your mind probably just isn't thinking along those lines.

But for simpler, short-term goals—I want to eat more healthy food, I want to make a B in biology this semester, I want to find a new job working 30 hours per week—the simple plan can be a simple way to stay on track.

Worksheet 2

One-Year Goal Worksheet

In one year, on ___/___/____, I want to:

_____

(Copy this form to use for several topics.)

The steps or mini-goals I will use to reach my goal are:

1._____

2._____

3._____

My Plan

Goal: _____ Deadline: _____

Mini-Goal #1: _____ Deadline: _____

   Step 1: _____

   Step 2: _____

   Step 3: _____

Mini-Goal #2: _____ Deadline: _____

   Step 1: _____

   Step 2: _____

   Step 3: _____

Mini-Goal #3: _____ Deadline: _____

   Step 1: _____

   Step 2: _____

   Step 3: _____

Resources

Carlson. R. (2000). *Don't sweat the small stuff for teens.* New York: Hyperion.

Davidson, J. (1997). *The complete idiot's guide to reaching your goals.* New York: Alpha Books.

Graham, S. (2000). *Teens can make it happen.* New York: Simon & Schuster.

McGraw, J. (2001). *Life strategies for teens.* New York: Fireside.

Top achievement. (n.d.). Retrieved December 13, 2002, from http://www.topachievement.com/.

Young, S. (2002). *Great failures of the extremely successful.* Los Angeles: Tallfellow Press.

CHAPTER 3

Teamwork
Finding the People Who
Will Support You

Y ou are going to need a lot of help to become independent. Maybe you thought being independent meant you didn't need anybody. But the truth is, nobody is truly independent. Even Henry David Thoreau, who became famous by living alone at Walden Pond and wrote a lot about independence, used an axe and tools made by other people. That's life.

Independence is hard work, and at times it can be frustrating, confusing, and even scary. When you get sick, what do you do about work? How do you know which colleges to apply for? Are you eligible for any kind of government aid? Who will cosign your lease? What if you suddenly think you've made a big mistake in attempting independence?

You need a *coaching team*. Your coaching team will help you figure out the answers to all of these questions and many more. This team is simply a group of people who will help you accomplish what you want to accomplish.

Your team will include mostly adults, since they are the ones who will have the experience and knowledge that you'll need. But friends are also an important part of this support system.

Let's figure out who should be on your team and why.

By the Numbers More than 100,000 kids in the United States call the National Runaway Switchboard each year (1-800-621-4000). Kids calling this crisis hotline have nobody else to turn to for the help or information they need. By setting up a good coaching team, you can avoid getting into a crisis situation.

The Help You Already Have

Chances are good that you already have some of your coaching team in place. Think of any adults you get along with well. Which ones, if any, can you tell the truth to about your life and your plans? Jot down a list of all the adults who might be able to help you in some way.

Now add a list of your close friends. These are the people you will keep in touch with even if you change schools or move to a new neighborhood.

Your list so far might have 15 names or just 3. The thing to remember is that you're not going to ask these people for huge favors. You're going to ask for help in small, manageable ways, depending on the areas that each person is useful in.

How Your Team Can Help

Now, I want you to imagine that you've just moved in to a new apartment, and the following horrible day happens to you:

> You wake up on a summer Monday morning with a scratchy throat. It feels like you're swallowing broken glass. But you haven't had time find a doctor yet, and you don't think you have any insurance. You stumble into the kitchen and drink some orange juice. Your head aches and you feel groggy, and you see your financial aid forms sitting on the table.

> You have to fill out the financial aid forms, but you don't understand half the questions. You have no idea what your parents' income is, and they won't tell you if you call to ask. You don't know what to put on the forms or who to call to ask about them.

> You sit there staring at the forms for an hour and a half, and then it's time to go to work. Cashiering and chatting with customers sounds like torture, but you can barely make your car payment as it is. You can't afford to take any time off work to stay home sick.

> You put your dirty work uniform back on, because you forgot to wash it. You drag yourself out to the street, start the car, and—nothing. Not a rumble, not a click. Not a sound. Your car is completely dead, and there's nobody around to give you a ride to work.

> You go back inside, and realize that you left your wallet in the car. You slam back outside to get it—can this day get any worse?—and lock yourself out of your apartment.

> You're stuck outside, locked out of your broken-down car, locked out of your apartment, feeling like crap, and late for work. You sit on the curb and cry.

Now, let's look at that day again, and see where a coaching team could help.

> You wake up on a summer Monday morning with a scratchy throat. It feels like you're swallowing broken glass. But you haven't had time to find a doctor yet, and you don't think you have any insurance. You call your aunt, a retired nurse, to get advice. She says you need a strep test and gives you the number of a local state health clinic. You call them and make an appointment for later that morning. You stumble into the kitchen and drink some orange juice. Your head aches and you feel groggy, and you see your financial aid forms sitting on the table.

You have to fill out the financial aid forms, but you don't understand half the questions. You have no idea what your parents' income is, and they won't tell you if you call to ask. You don't know what to put on the forms or who to call to ask about it. You call your guidance counselor, who has agreed to answer your questions even over the summer. She tells you to call the financial aid officer of the college and explain. You do this and also tell the financial aid officer that you're sick. You make an appointment to go there in three days to get help in person.

Then it's time to go to work. Cashiering and chatting with customers sounds like torture, but you can barely make your car payment as it is. You can't afford to take any time off work to stay home sick.

You put back on your dirty work uniform, because you forgot to wash it. (Hey, coaching teams can't work miracles. Do your laundry!) You drag yourself out to the street, start the car, and—nothing. Not a rumble, not a click. Not a sound. Your car is completely dead, and there's nobody around to give you a ride to work. You call your sister, and she agrees to come over and try to jump start your car so you can get it to the auto repair shop. She suggests that you call your boss, explain your problems, and see if you can switch work days. You call him, and he is able to sign you up for a half-day later in the week so that at least you don't lose all your hours.

You go back inside, and realize that you left your wallet in the car. You slam back outside to get it—can this day get any worse?—and lock yourself out of your apartment. You borrow the extra key you've left with the old lady down the hall. (Neighbors who are home a lot make good coaching team members.)

When you get inside, you call a good friend for a pep talk. He agrees to take you to pick up your car the next day if you take it to a repair shop. You drink some hot tea and wait for your sister to arrive. After dropping off the car at the shop, she takes you to your doctor's appointment and then back home. You take your medicine, crawl into bed, and sleep.

So, can your coaching team get your car fixed for free, make your strep throat disappear, and fill our your financial aid forms for you? Of course not. But they can make a tremendously rotten day bearable, and they can make an okay day fantastic.

Each person's coaching team will be different. Some kids have large groups of friends and family members to call on for help, whereas others aren't speaking to their family and don't have many friends. Some kids will have a team made up of people they've known for years, and others will only meet their coaching team because they're trying to live independently.

Who is on your team and how long you've known them doesn't matter that much. The key is coming up with people who can help you, even in small ways, when you need it.

Look at the list of names you've jotted down. Beside each name, write down what you think they could help you with. A friend can help with letting you blow off steam, just hanging out and relaxing, maybe giving you a ride somewhere, going with you to a doctor's appointment you don't want to go to alone, and so on. You might have a sister-in-law you don't see all that much, but who is a realtor. She can answer your questions about leases and maybe help you look at apartments. Even if that's not something you'd ordinarily do together, you might find her willing to help. Maybe a friend's older brother is an auto mechanic. He might be willing to come over and put a new battery in your car in exchange for a large pizza and soda (plus the cost of the battery, of course), saving you $50 in labor charges.

The point is, think about what each person on your list is good at. Also, jot down when they're available. If your brother is a teacher, you are not going to be able to call on him with daytime problems unless it's a real emergency. It's good to have an idea of when the people on your team work, and when it's okay to call them.

How Can Your Team Help You?

You can use support in every area of your life. Here are a few areas where you might want help:

Transportation
- Buying a car
- Cosigning a purchase
- Giving you rides if your car is in the shop or if you do not have a car
- Helping you learn how to use the mass transit system in your area

Work
- Talking about careers
- Creating a resume
- Practicing for job interviews

School
- Filling out college applications
- Studying for the SAT or GED
- Helping with financial aid questions and paperwork
- Visiting schools with you

Home
- Choosing an apartment
- Looking over leases
- Cosigning a lease
- Showing you maintenance stuff (like how to make the toilet stop running)

Financial stuff
- Helping with taxes
- Answering questions about your budget

Medical
- Advising you on whether you need to see a doctor
- Figuring out if you have insurance
- Helping you find insurance
- Accompanying you to your doctor's appointment

Life stuff
- Listening to you when you vent
- Having fun together
- Discussing big decisions

Ten Possibilities for Your Support Team

1. Older brothers and sisters
2. Other adult family members
3. Guidance counselor
4. School social worker
5. Boss
6. Teacher
7. Neighbor at your new place
8. Mentor
9. Friends
10. Minister

Building Your Support Team

With most adults, it will work out best if you ask them ahead of time if they are willing to help. The easiest approach is to be simple and honest. For example, you might say to your sister-in-law who is a realtor, "Janet, I know I don't see you very often, but I'm wondering if you'd be willing to help me find an apartment when I move out. I don't know what to look for, and I'm not sure how to read a lease." Or, to your guidance counselor, "Mr. Bowman, I'm going to be moving out of the house this summer. Would you be willing to give me advice about social services and school issues and answer questions for me as I have them?"

Asking people in advance will make it easier when you actually need help. Instead of calling in a panic and having to explain the long story of how you've moved out, your parents aren't helping with college applications or financial aid, and so on, you can go right to, "Hi, Mr. Bowman. Thanks for agreeing to help me out over the summer. I have a list of questions about college and financial aid. Do you have a few minutes, or should I call back later?"

People are more willing to help when the guidelines are laid down up front. For example, if Mr. Bowman has agreed to answer questions and you call asking him for a ride to work, warning buzzers are going to go off in his head, and he'll probably say no. He will be worried that you are going to keep asking for more and more. But if your sister is a stay-at-home mom and has agreed to give you rides to work when you are without transportation, then she will probably say yes.

How to Ask for Help

Asking someone from your team (or anybody, for that matter) for help can be tough. After all, you crave independence, so asking for help may be something you are not used to. But it's really not that hard. Here are some tips:

- **Be specific.** If you are calling to ask for a ride, make sure you know the exact time you need the ride and where you need to go. Let the person know whether you'd like them to just drop you off or if you need a ride back home, too.
- **Avoid excuses.** Don't come up with a list of excuses. If you fail a test and whine about it, most teachers will see that as not taking responsibility for your actions. Just explain that you need help with the class and ask about tutoring or study groups.
- **Be polite.** Adults put up with just as much crap from people as you do, and they don't like it any better. A little politeness will take you a long way toward getting help. Maybe you are frustrated with financial aid forms and say, "How am I supposed to know what this means?" The financial aid officer will probably help you, but he's not going to go the extra mile for you. But try saying, "I'm sorry I haven't filled out this paperwork, but I don't understand all the questions. Can you help me?" The financial aid officer is a lot more likely to walk you step by step through the form until it's all filled out correctly.

- **Be adult about it.** Don't try to guilt people into helping by begging or acting pathetic. There is nothing wrong with asking for help (as long as you don't repeatedly take advantage of someone), but there's nothing wrong with people saying no, either. Your guidance counselor may have another appointment when you want to talk, or your neighbor might not be home when you wanted her to sign for a delivery for you. Remember, your team is not obligated to do whatever you ask. They are resources who have agreed to help you when they can. The great thing about a big coaching team is that you probably have someone else to ask.
- **Say thank you.** You'd be surprised how many people don't hear that enough.

How to Keep Your Support Team Happy

So, you've got this great group of adults and friends who are willing to help you in your journey toward independence. Now you need to keep them happy enough to keep helping you. You want to keep their friendship, too. There are two main things you can do: Avoid taking advantage of people, and be appreciative.

Calling your aunt who's a nurse to see if you should see the doctor about a scratchy throat is not taking advantage of her. Calling her every hour to report that your temperature has gone up one-tenth of a degree; asking her to buy and bring over throat lozenges, call and make a doctor's appointment for you, and then take you to the doctor; and, oh by the way, could she do those dishes in the sink…That's taking advantage!

People will be willing to help you if you are reasonable. Don't call your guidance counselor every single day with little questions. Save them up for a week and make one phone call so that you don't waste his or her time. Don't expect one friend to drive you to work every day for two weeks. Ask a few different friends, so nobody is doing too much work for you.

Remember, everybody has busy lives. We all have work and relationships. Other people are not put on earth simply to help you. Try to be reasonable about what you expect others to do for you.

Which brings us to the second thing. When people do things for you, be appreciative! It shouldn't be that hard, because you do appreciate it, right? I'm not saying you need to send Hallmark cards and flowers to everyone who helps you, but you can do some simple things that will let them know you appreciate their help.

Saying thank you is the easiest. This has even more effect if you say thanks at the time—as they drop you off at work, for instance—and then again later. If your friend gave you rides all week, give her a call that weekend to chat and thank her one more time for going out of her way every day. If your brother-in-law helped you go car shopping, call or e-mail him the next day with a thanks.

Another way to show appreciation is to not blow your opportunities. In other words, if Aunt Rita goes to the trouble of making that phone call to get you a doctor's appointment, *go* to the appointment. If your teacher gives you an extra credit opportunity at your request, do a good job at it. If people go out of their way to help you with something and then you blow it off, you are saying you don't really care about the trouble they went to. This is a sure way to make someone unwilling to help you next time.

Another great way to show thanks is to share the results with the person who helped you. When a guidance counselor helps you with the college application process, call, e-mail, or drop by to show off that acceptance letter. He or she will be thrilled. When your brother-in-law helps you research cars, drive by to let him see the car after you get it.

You could also return someone's favor. If your sister gives you a ride while your car is in the shop, offer her a few bucks toward gas. If your neighbor has signed for seven packages and let you back into your apartment twice this month (you've got to stop locking yourself out!), offer to walk her dog when she's sick, or bake her some cookies.

Of course, there are lots of ways to show you appreciate people. They don't have to take a lot of effort on your part, but it is important to do something to let people know you're thankful for their help.

My Support Team List

As you build your coaching team, keep track of their information on a support team worksheet (see Worksheet 3). It is good to have addresses for everyone, because you might need to use some of them for references for job and school applications. Make several copies and keep one by the phone, one in your wallet, one in the car, and one anywhere else that will be handy. When something comes up that you need help with or advice on, you will have a list of resources at your fingertips, all of people willing to help you!

Stuck in the Middle

It is hard to keep people in your family happy members of your coaching team, but ways to do it exist. Don't put your other family members in the middle of your issues with your parents. Don't ask them to take sides or keep big secrets for you if they still

Getting Services from Your State

State governments offer assistance for some teens trying to live independently, usually, but not always, teens already in the system due to parental abuse or neglect. That aid can be in the form of low-income housing, special education and job training programs, health care, and much more. The problem is that not the same department in every state administers these programs, so it can be tough to figure out who to call.

Check out http://www.acf.hhs.gov/programs/ocs/ssbg/docs/stoff.htm on the U.S. Department of Health and Human Services' website. It lists a name, address, phone number, and often an e-mail address of the person in each state who should be able to direct you to the right person to answer your specific questions.

If you don't have access to the Web, look in the blue pages of your phone book under state government, and then look for an agency with a name like Social Services, Family and Children's Services, or Children's Welfare.

When you contact somebody in the social services field, be ready with some specific questions. You might say, "I'm 17 and living on my own. I'm working full-time and trying to stay in school. I'm wondering if there are any programs that might help me with low-income housing, job training, or transportation." If you clarify to yourself what kind of help you need, social workers and government employees will be better able to help you.

Worksheet 3

My Support Team

NAME	PHONE	E-MAIL	ADDRESS	AREAS OF HELP	NOTES

have a good relationship with your mom and dad. Try to build your own relationship with them, and just avoid the topic of your parents, if necessary.

I will never forget the day I got my key stuck in my older sister's front door lock. I was 16, and I was staying with her for a few months while I saved up money for an apartment and school. My parents had dropped by to convince her not to let me live with her. I stood there, jiggling the key, for what seemed like hours, listening to my parents badmouth me in the next room. I didn't know until then how much pressure she was getting from my parents not to help me. She did anyway, which made all the difference.

She wanted to get along with everybody, and I hated the situation I was putting her in. I tried never to make her feel like it was them or me, never to make her feel guilty for still seeing or talking to our parents, even if I wasn't. Don't make it too uncomfortable for your sisters, brothers, grandparents, aunts, and uncles to help you. Don't insist that they see your side of everything. Accept that they can have good relationships with your parents and still support you in your independence.

Resources: National Crisis Hotlines

If you are out of the house already or in a crisis situation and don't know where to turn, call one of these national hotline numbers.

AIDS Teen Hotline
1-800-234-TEEN (1-800-234-8336)

1:30 P.M.–8:00 P.M. Central Standard Time, Monday through Friday

You can leave a message at any time.

Al-Anon/Alateen Hotline
1-800-344-2666 (United States); 1-800-443-4525 (Canada)

8:00 A.M.–6:00 P.M. Eastern Standard Time, Monday through Friday

Provides information and meeting details for kids who have alcohol problems or who have family members with alcohol problems.

America's Pregnancy Helpline
1-888-467-8466

7:30 A.M.–10:00 P.M. Central Standard Time, Monday through Friday

Has counselors and varied weekend hours. You can leave a message at any time.

Childhelp USA's National Child Abuse Hotline
1-800-422-4453—24 hours a day

Children of the Night
1-800-551-1300—24 hours a day

Short-term crisis help for kids involved in prostitution or pornography.

Covenant House Nineline
1-800-999-9999

24-hour national crisis hotline for youth younger than 21 and their families. Staff can refer you to local agencies to help.

Girls and Boys Town National Crisis Line
1-800-448-3000—24 hours a day

National Life Center Hotline/Pregnancy Hotline
1-800-848-5683—24 hours per day

National Runaway Switchboard
1-800-621-4000—24 hours per day

You do not have to be a runaway to call this number. Staff will answer questions for you about teen issues and will help you find resources in your area.

The Trevor Project
1-800-850-8078

24-hour suicide prevention hotline for gay youth.

United Way's First Call for Help
211

The phone number of 211 is available in some parts of the country as the direct line to United Way's First Call for Help, or try http://national.unitedway.org/help/. This can be a great resource if you do not know who to call about issues like housing, insurance, safety, mental and physical health, and so on. The counselors on the phone will refer you to the local resources that can help you. If 211 does not work in your area, log on to the website to find your local number, or call information, 411, and ask for the local United Way number.

Lessons

Does School Train You for Real Life?

*I*f you spend your time worrying about making the rent, fixing your car, or staying awake on the job, going to high school might feel like a waste of time. After all, what good is knowing Steinbeck's *The Grapes of Wrath* going to do you when you are selling jackets at 25% off for six hours a day?

The answer is, it might not do you any good—right this minute. But if you look back at Chapter 2 at the goals you set for yourself, you'll see why staying in school is the right decision.

By the Numbers

Education and Income

Want proof of what Steinbeck or geometry means to your life?
Check out these average annual incomes from 1998 of people older than 25:

No high school diploma $19,200

High school diploma 26,000

Some college, no degree 30,400

Associate's degree 31,700

Bachelor's degree 40,100

It doesn't get much simpler than this: More education equals more money. You might not see the money right away, because with just a high school diploma, you usually start out at the bottom of the ladder and work your way up. But without that diploma, you might end up sitting on that bottom rung for good.

27

The truth is that the geometry you are learning may or may not have anything to do with your daily life at this point, but if you want to create a successful life, a high school diploma is usually a necessary stepping stone. Sure, you've heard of those celebrities who never finished high school, and look how famous and rich they are. But they are absolutely the minority. For every celebrity with no diploma that you read about, there are thousands of average people who are living on the streets or are just scraping by because they cannot get a good job. And why not? At least partly because they didn't finish high school.

Do You Need to Stay in School?

Answer the following questions with a true or false.

1. I am 16 years old or older.

2. I do not plan to attend college.

3. I plan to join the military.

4. I know what career I want to have and how much training it requires.

5. I am getting financial support from someone who expects me to continue attending school.

6. My career choice requires a four-year degree.

7. My career choice requires a certification or licensing course.

Now check out your score. For Numbers 1, 2, and 4, give yourself one point for true and two points for false. For Numbers 3, 5, 6, and 7, give yourself two points for true and one point for false. Now add up your points.

0–7 Ready to get out?—Maybe you are one of the few people who do not need a high school diploma right now. That doesn't mean it wouldn't be a good thing to have, of course.

8+ Stay in!—If you scored 8 or more, you have a very good reason to keep attending high school. High school is the best way to accomplish your goals, whether they include the military or some other career that requires training.

If You Cannot Stay in School

What if you cannot stay in school? Maybe you have a child, or you have to work 40 hours a week right now and can't handle the classwork, but you know that you don't want to cut off all your options. What can you do?

You can take the GED test. If you pass it, you will receive your GED. In general, a GED will keep your options open for you. Students who pass the GED can enter the military, apply to college, and qualify for certification courses in most fields. In fact, some research shows that kids who pass the GED often go on to perform better in these programs than the average high school graduate.

But, and this is a big but, if you don't plan on any further education or training, a GED is not considered as good as a diploma.

In other words, if you get your GED and then go to college and graduate, that college graduation is what your future employers will care about, not that you left school at 17 and got your GED. But if you just earn your GED and do nothing more, your GED will not be as respected as a high school diploma. Some researchers say that employers see the GED as a sign that the student wouldn't stick it out.

A GED is certainly better than nothing, but a diploma is a little bit better than a GED, in terms of income earned and respect gained.

Taking the GED Test

The GED test is offered at more than 3,000 sites in the United States and Canada. Call 1-800-626-9433 and request the basic information packet. It will tell you the closest exam sites, the schedule, and all the other information you need.

GED consists of five subject areas. The sections cover writing, including an essay; reading; social studies; science; and mathematics. The five tests take a total of seven hours and five minutes. Some testing sites make you take the entire test in one or two sessions. Others let you come in and take one subject area at a time.

To find a course to help you prepare for the exam, check the yellow pages under schools. Look for adult education programs. If you cannot find one, call the local high school or library and ask for help.

GED Connection is a study program that airs on public television stations nationwide. Check Literacy Link at http://litlink.ket.org/ to see if your local station is running them soon. Tape them to play back and study later. This website also offers free online pretests and lessons.

Many adult education and tutoring companies offer GED courses, but they cost money. Some are very inexpensive, and others are not. Be sure you find out how many classes are offered, which subjects are covered, how much time you are expected to study outside of class, and what the class costs before you sign up.

Do You Need to Go to College?

We've talked about staying in high school versus dropping out versus taking your GED. What if high school isn't the question, but college is?

As you saw in the income figures, a college degree generally equals a bigger income. But maybe you are sick of school, or you don't know how you'd pay for it, or you don't even know what you want to be. How do you decide whether to make the effort or not?

Well, one way to make the decision is to look at your career goals, if you already know them. If your dream job is accounting or veterinary medicine or teaching, then you almost certainly will need a college degree. What other careers require a four-year degree or more?

Most professional businesspeople need four-year degrees. Accountants, bankers, scientists, engineers, doctors, pharmacists, business managers, therapists, psychologists, attorneys…all of these careers and many more usually require at least a bachelor's degree. Do exceptions exist? Yes, in some cases a person might be doing the technical work of an engineer or a scientist without having at least a four-year-degree. But chances are that without the degree, that person is not getting the pay he or she deserves. That is the case with two friends of mine who have on-the-job training and work as engineers, but do not have college degrees.

College is no longer an all or nothing prospect. If you are sick of school, really, horribly, can't-stand-to-take-another-test sick of it, why not take a semester or a year off? Independence will be challenging enough without stressing yourself out more. Or, go to college part-time. Increasingly, kids paying their own way through college work full-time and go to school part-time, taking just a couple of classes each semester.

And if you know that you want to attend college, but you don't know what career you want, get started anyway. Many classes are required of all students no matter what their major. These are often called general education requirements, and you can take them first. Some topic might really light your fire, and if none does, make an appointment with the school's vocational counselor to talk about what you might like to do for a career.

If you know that you do not want to go to college right now, keep the option in mind in the coming years. Now that people of all ages attend college, it's really not a big deal to start college in your 20s or older. You might not fit in quite as well, but chances are, as you grow up and live independently, you will find that fitting in isn't as important as it used to be.

TOP 10 Ten Great Careers Requiring One Year of Training or Less

Many more jobs than these do not require college degrees. The following are some examples that show you it is possible to build a career, even a well-paying one, without that four-year degree. Keep in mind, however, that most of these positions do require some training program after high school.

1. Appliance and electrical equipment servicepeople
2. Salespeople
3. Fire fighters
4. Science technicians
5. Transportation workers
6. Plumbers
7. Bricklayers
8. Truck drivers
9. Realtors
10. Auto mechanics

TOP 10 Ten Resources for Paying for College and Post–High School Programs

1. Relatives
2. Job with an education benefit (some companies will pay for your education)
3. Grants
4. Scholarships
5. Your jobs
6. Savings account
7. Programs offered by your state's education or social services department
8. Military/Reserve Officers Training Corps program
9. Church/religious charities
10. Student loans

The hardest thing about starting college after a break is that you do forget a lot of what you learned in high school, and you get out of the studying habit. When I taught 8th-grade English, I took a college night course in literature to earn the credits I needed to keep my teaching license. I had only been out of college for about two years, but I really struggled with getting back into the habit of taking notes and studying.

How Can You Afford College if You Are Broke?

If you really want to attend college, you can. That's the most important thing I want to tell you. It's the bottom line. Don't skip college because you think you can't afford it. It might take incredibly hard work, and you might rack up lots of loans to pay back, but you can go.

There are many kinds of financial aid that can help you pay for college. The following is just a brief overview of some of the most common types.

- **Student loans.** Student loans are, just as the name says, loans. You have to pay them back. But you don't begin repaying until six months or so after you graduate, and the interest rate is low. Loans have limits on how much you can borrow per year.
- **Grants.** Groups sometimes award grants to those with financial need. They may be awarded by the school, by the government, or by an organization. You do not ever have to repay grants.
- **Scholarships.** You also do not have to pay back scholarships. Sometimes scholarships are based on financial need, but other times they are awarded for certain academic or athletic achievements.
- **Military aid.** The armed services offer many programs in which the military pays your tuition in exchange for military service.
- **Service programs.** Some organizations, like National Civilian Community Corps and Volunteers in Service to America, offer money toward tuition or payment of student loans, in exchange for a period of voluteerism.
- **Jobs/work-study.** Some schools offer programs in which students who demonstrate financial need get first consideration for on-campus jobs. These are great jobs to have, because having your school and work in the same place simplifies your life.

Many kinds of financial aid exist; this is a very complicated area. The best thing to do is to make an appointment with a financial aid advisor at the school you will be attending. Explain your living situation and your financial situation. Be honest about both, and don't be embarrassed to let them see a little desperation! Ask him or her to help you figure out what types of aid you might qualify for. Additional aid packages are available to people of a certain age, religion, gender, career choice, ethnic background, and much more. You need to talk to an expert in this area to make sure that you take advantage of all the financial aid for which you qualify.

Make sure that a student loan is your last resort. You probably will need to get one, but do not automatically apply for the full amount. Remember, loaned money is not a gift, and the less you have to pay back, the better!

How to Navigate the Financial Aid Maze

First, make an appointment with an expert. Take a spiral notebook with pockets, write Financial Aid on the cover, and don't use it for anything else. Bring the notebook to the appointment. Make sure you know your income, your rent, and your legal status—are you emancipated? Are you just living independently? Your legal status can affect what kinds of financial aid you are eligible for. If you have a monthly budget, bring it.

In your notebook, make a list of anything that might open up certain aid areas for you. What is your ethnic background or heritage? What is your religion? What do you plan to major in? Are you interested in doing military service in exchange for tuition? Do you plan on attending school full-time or part-time? Also, make sure you have your social security number with you, plus a sheet with your coaching team information on it. If you filled out a tax form last year, bring a copy of that, too.

Write down the name and phone number of the financial aid advisor in your notebook. Ask if he or she is who you should call when you have questions.

During your appointment, take notes. Jot down what the advisor thinks are the most likely sources of aid for you. Take any handouts he or she gives you and put them in your notebook. Find out what your next step should be. Also, find out if each step of the process has a particular deadline. For example, if she tells you to fill out the FAFSA form, ask her what date you should turn it in by. Write the date in your notebook.

Criteria for Independent Status for Financial Aid

Long ago, students were independent if they were not claimed as dependents on someone's tax returns for two years. *This is no longer true.* The Federal Need Analysis Methodology currently determines a student to be independent if any of the following are true:

1. Student is 24 years old or older as of December 31 of the award year.

2. Student is a graduate or professional student.

3. Student is married.

4. Student has children or dependents other than a spouse who receive more than half their support from the student and will continue to do so through the end of the award year.

5. Student is an orphan or ward of the court, or was a ward of the court through age 18.

6. Student is a veteran of the U.S. Armed Forces.

See http://www.finaid.org/calculators/dependency.phtml for more details.

If you do not fit these criteria, you can appeal your dependency status by asking for a professional judgment review by the financial aid administrator at your college or university. Provide as much independent third-party documentation of your circumstances as possible, such as court orders or reports from social workers and clergy that document an estranged or abusive relationship with your parents. FinAid has a section devoted to this topic: http://www.finaid.org/otheraid/parentsrefuse.phtml.

—*Mark Kantrowitz*
Publisher of FinAid.org

Expert Advice: Financial Aid

1. The sooner you start, the better off you will be. Start searching for scholarships and saving for college as early as possible.

2. If you do not expect to attend college immediately, look into establishing a section 529 college savings plan for yourself (see www.finaid.org/savings/ for details). This is a tax-advantaged way of saving for college. You could work for several years, building up college savings, and then apply for college when you turn 24.

3. Even if your parents will not help you pay for college, try to convince them to sign the Free Application for Federal Student Aid (FAFSA) form. Point out that signing it does not mean they have to give you any financial support, but does enable you to borrow a Stafford Loan in your own name.

4. Search for scholarships using a free scholarship search service, such as FastWeb.com, the largest free scholarship search tool. Do not spend money to search for scholarships, apply for a scholarships, or apply for loans. If you have to pay money to get money, it's probably a scam.

5. Be organized. Maintain separate file folders for each scholarship, college admissions application, and college financial aid application. This is a large, complex project. Do not underestimate the amount of time it will take. Watch those deadlines. Keep checklists so that you know what has been sent out and what has not, and when everything is due. Try to get things done early, instead of waiting until the last minute.

6. If you do not have parental support, ask the colleges to waive the admissions application fees (typically $20–$60 each). This will save you some money and give you some early practice jumping through the hoops necessary to get the financial aid administrator to override your default dependency status.

7. Keep photocopies of every application and every document. That way, if an application is lost in the mail, you can quickly make another copy to resubmit.

8. Get a certificate of mailing when you mail an application, as it gives you proof of the date the application was mailed. If your FAFSA was lost in the mail, for example, causing you to miss the state deadline, the certificate of mailing can help you try to retain the by-the-deadline priority for state aid.

9. If an award requires you to be nominated by your school, find out who decides which students are nominated, and ask him or her to nominate you. If the nomination deadline is approaching, often he or she will nominate you because you were the only one to ask. In other cases, the school will have a formal process by which students are selected, but it doesn't hurt to ask.

10. Learn about the tax credits for education, such as the Hope Scholarship, the Lifetime Learning Tax Credit, and student loan interest tax deduction, as many of these credits are available to the person who pays the education bills, which in this case would be you.

—Mark Kantrowitz
Publisher of FinAid.org

Community College Versus Four-year College

Community colleges are two-year schools. At a community college, you can earn an associate's degree of arts or sciences, or you might earn a specific certification, like a medical transcription or computer repair certificate. You can also proceed on to a four-year-college after earning your associate's degree, and the classes you took at the community college will, for the most part, transfer as credits toward your bachelor's degree.

The United States has almost 1,200 community colleges, and more than 10 million students attend them. Part-time students are more common in community colleges than in four-year schools. Health care and technology are two of the most popular fields for community-college students.

Although some kids feel a stigma is attached to community colleges, that only those who can't cut a "real" college go, this is untrue. Plenty of people build very successful careers after attending community colleges. Whether a community college is the right choice for you depends largely on the kind of career you hope to build. Also, many students enjoy the smaller campuses and class sizes of community colleges.

Talk to a guidance counselor at your local high school, if you can. If not, call your local community college and make an appointment to talk to someone in the admissions office or in the counseling and advising office. Be ready to discuss your goals, your questions, and your concerns when you meet with that person. Then, talk over your options with a trusted person from your coaching team. As you talk it out, you will probably know in your gut what is the right decision for you.

When you get home, write that date down on your calendar or tack a sign on your refrigerator. One of the keys to receiving financial aid is to simply do the paperwork correctly and on time. When you do not understand the forms, open up your notebook and call the financial advisor back. That person's job is to answer your questions, so don't be afraid to ask.

As you go through the financial aid process (and it is a process, not just an hour-long meeting!), make sure you ask these questions about each kind of aid possibility:

- Do I have to pay this back? (If so, get the repayment schedule, interest rate, etc.)
- What grade point average do I have to maintain?
- Do I have to be a full-time student to receive this aid?
- Is it automatically renewed each year or semester, or do I have to apply again?

In addition to meeting with your college financial aid advisor, also talk with the career counselor from your high school. He or she might know of other very specific awards, contests, or scholarships for which you might be eligible.

Getting into College

I am not really going to address choosing a college, because the truth is that most independent teens are so broke that they pretty much choose whatever college is closest to them. If you have a special skill that will earn you a scholarship, or if you really want to move to another area of the country, go for it. But generally, most kids will be simply checking to make sure that the college closest to home offers a degree program in their area of interest.

If you are feeling more adventurous than that, please talk to the guidance counselor at your high school. Or if that is not an option, check to see if the biggest library nearby has a librarian who could help you sort out some of your choices.

So, you've decided you want to go to college. Now, how do you get in?

First, pick up the application packet from the college, read it carefully, and go from there.

Second, make sure you've taken the SAT exam. You probably took it as an 11th-grader. If not, you need to call the high school and ask the guidance counselor how you can take it, visit http://www.collegeboard.com for more information, or call the Educational Testing Service at 619/771-7600 for information and registration materials.

Third, you will need transcripts from your high school. This is an official copy of all the classes you took and the grades you received. Most colleges will want your high school to send the transcript directly to them. You will need to call or write your high school to get this done.

Fourth, fill out the application. Applying to college is a lot of paperwork, and you will need to write at least one essay. Be honest about your plans, hopes, and goals for your life and why you want to attend college. Have someone on your coaching team proofread your essay for you before you send it in.

Fifth, get letters of reference, if you need them. These are letters from adults you know talking about your good qualities. You should ask at least three adults, if you can, to write you letters of recommendation. These might be teachers, bosses, or adults from your coaching team.

Next, send everything to the college on time. Again, put the deadlines on your calendar or hang that big sign on the fridge.

Each college application is a little bit different, so make sure that you follow the directions in your application packet. If you don't understand something, call the admissions office and ask for a better explanation. Some colleges and universities offer online applications, so check out that possibility if that appeals to you.

Applying to college can be tedious, especially if you are applying at lots of colleges, but grit your teeth and get it done. Universities are getting pickier because more students are applying, so if there are several in your area, apply to all of them.

Making the Grade

All right, you've decided to stay in or go back to school! Now what? Well, you are working hard, whether it's high school or college. So follow these tips to make sure you are not wasting your time.

Half of life is just showing up. Don't cut classes. This may be easier to remember in college, when you are actually writing out checks to pay for those classes. But whether it's college or high school, attending class is the easiest way to stay on top of things.

Participate. Try to really listen to what the teacher says. Ask questions when you don't understand. You deserve a good education. Do what you need to get it. Take notes.

Get organized. Have a place to study at home. Have a spot for your books, and keep any due dates for projects and quizzes or test dates on a big calendar. Try to set up a study routine. Even 10 minutes a day of review for each class (each class, not just the ones you attended that day) can really pay off. When you have a big project or paper, break it down into small pieces and set yourself a deadline for each piece. That way, you won't have to stay up for 72 hours straight just before it's due to finish it.

If you are struggling, try to get help. Ask about a tutor. See if you can meet the professor before school or during office hours. Form a study group with a few other kids from class. Ask if there are supplemental materials that might help you (videos, tapes, etc.).

Keep looking ahead. Sometimes school might feel unimportant, not worth the hassle. But keep looking down the road at your long-term goals. Want to be a computer technician? Maybe you need that high school diploma to enter the certificate program for computer tech. So, even though cell biology might not matter to you personally, it does matter to you as far as getting what you want. Try to keep in mind why your classes are important to you, even the ones you can't stand.

Resources

Books

Many publishers, including Random House, Barron's, ARCO, and McGraw-Hill, put out a new GED study book every year. Check your library or local bookstore for the most updated version available. In addition, new SAT study guides come out every year.

Buxton, T. (2002). *The secret to your college success: 101 ways to make the most of your college experience*. Campbell, CA: Writers Club Press.

Kaplan, B. R. (2001). *How to go to college almost for free*. New York: HarperCollins.

Laurenzo, P. V. (2002). *College financial aid: How to get your fair share*. Albany, NY: Hudson Financial Press.

Robson, J. B. (2001). *Beginning college 101: How to achieve real success in college*. New Brunswick, NJ: College and Future.

Spethman, M. J. (1997). *High school bound: The ultimate guide for high school success and survival*. Miami, FL: Westgate.

Hotlines

Federal Student Aid Information Center hotline
1-800-4-FED-AID

GED hotline
1-800-626-9433 (or call your state's Department of Education)

Websites

Bureau of Labor Statistics
http://www.bls.gov/k12/html/edu_over.htm
Basic career info from the Bureau of Labor Statistics

Center for Adult Learning and Educational Credentials (official GED site)
http://www.acenet.edu/calec/ged/

College Board
http://www.collegeboard.com/
SAT information from College Board

FAFSA
http://www.fafsa.ed.gov
Free Application for Federal Student Aid

FinAid

http://www.finaid.org/

The SmartStudent™ Guide to Financial Aid

PBS

http://www.litlink.ket/org/

Free GED practice and resource materials from PBS

Steck-Vaughn's GED Practice

http://www.harcourtachieve.com/ and click on the GED practice link

Free GED practice exam questions from Steck-Vaughn publishing company

CHAPTER 5

Going Pro
Choosing the Right Job or Career

So, you are out of the house and ready to start your life. The question is, What are you planning to do with it? Direct movies? Play bass in a rock band? Run your own company? Are you going to leave home and step right into the lifestyle of your dreams?

Unlikely. I don't say this to discourage you, but chances are, the jobs you will take to pay the rent and buy food will not bear much resemblance to your dream job.

But that's okay. The jobs you work at over the next few years while you build your independent life don't need to be dream jobs; however, they do need to take you one step closer to those dreams. Work life for the next few years is probably going to consist of flipping burgers, selling blouses, typing letters, or loading trucks. That's not a bad thing. Although you might not want to flip burgers forever (and who does?), that might be one necessary step on your way to directing movies.

How's that? Well, look at it logically. Say you want to direct movies one day. What will you need to do that? Do a little research and you will find out that attending film school is your best route, because then you'll not only learn the skills you need, but you'll also have access to the school's equipment, which is way too expensive for you to purchase on your own. To attend film school, you are going to need financial aid and hopefully will get some scholarships. To qualify for that, you need to keep up your high school grades. To keep up your grades, you need a job that offers flexible hours, is close to home, and pays enough for you to make the rent.

Flipping burgers might be it.

Dropping fries and nuking danishes might not seem like the job you really want, but if you see it as step one on your road to becoming a movie director, it can be a little easier to take.

The difference between your short-term job and your dream job is that your short-term job is one you are doing right now to accomplish your most immediate goals—having food to eat, money to pay the bills, and time to study so that you graduate with good grades. Once you accomplish these immediate goals, you move on to your next goals. Maybe, in college, a goal might be to get any kind of job in a film production company. Will you be directing movies yet? No. But again, it's one step on the road to your dream job.

Teen Jobs

Unfortunately, the jobs most often available to teens tend to be kind of boring. Why is that? Well, teens change jobs frequently, so they tend to get hired for jobs that don't require a lot of training. Companies don't want to spend four months training employees who are likely to change jobs every semester.

The jobs also tend to be not very challenging and not require much responsibility. The reason for that one is that unfortunately, a lot of teens don't show much responsibility on the job, trying instead to get by with doing the least amount of work possible. I can promise, though, if you are responsible, your boss will find a way to give you more responsibility. And if he or she doesn't, ask for some.

Also, teen jobs tend to be retail (selling stuff) and service jobs (such as restaurants) because those businesses are open nights and weekends, when most teens are available to work. Businesses that run on a 9 A.M. to 5 P.M. schedule don't have teen employees because teens are in school during most of those hours.

Finding a Job

There are plenty of ways to find jobs. First, take into account what your job must have. Does it need to be close enough to ride a bike to? If you are still in school during weekdays, the business must be open evenings and weekends. Have you figured out a minimum hourly amount you must make to pay your bills? Check your monthly budget carefully to make sure you have not left anything out, then divide that amount by the number of hours you are able to work per month. That is the amount you need to make *after taxes* to pay all your bills. Multiply that amount by 1.25 to get the approximately amount you will need to make before taxes are taken out.

Once you have thought about what needs your job must meet, you can start looking. Help wanted signs are an easy way to find a job, and so is checking the classified ads—Sundays in the print paper, or at any time in online classified ads. Word of mouth is another way. Tell all your friends and the adults on your coaching team that you are job hunting. Let them know what kind of job you are interested in. You never know who will have a connection that will come in handy. You also might find a job through a government program like Job Corps, which offers education and job training to economically disadvantaged kids.

Also, check with your high school about Department of Education and Cultural Affairs (DECA) work programs. These are run by each state's DECA office. They offer paid internships or jobs that can sometimes be worked during school hours and for which you can receive high school credit. Some programs also count as credit toward a post-high-school certificate or license.

Another way to find a job is to approach a place that you really like. I have one niece who has a cute little pizza place all picked out for her first job when she turns 16. She just loves the atmosphere there and wants it to be her first real job. I know guys who got their first jobs at auto parts stores because they felt comfortable and knowledgeable there, and several girls whose first real jobs were selling clothes at their favorite shops. Do be careful about working someplace you really like to buy things, because it's tempting to spend your entire paycheck where you work. I love books, and a bookstore was one of my early jobs. They did not have a help wanted sign up, but I just went to every bookstore in the couple of malls close to home and filled out applications.

Job Scams

A job scam is a job that is too good to be true. Most job scams aimed at young people work like this: You see an ad that says, "Work from home! Set your own hours! Make $10,000 per month working PART-TIME! Call 1-888-YOU-LOSE for more information."

Sounds perfect, right? So, you call the toll-free number and get a recording, telling you all about your great new career in international marketing, sales, medical billing, restaurant testing, or whatever the latest gimmick is. Then it tells you that all you have to do to start your great new job is send $15 to an address, and they will send you everything you need to get started.

So you send the $15, and you wait. And you wait.

Sometimes, you won't ever get anything in exchange for your money.

Other times, you'll get a packet of information about your new "job," plus a list of people to contact for work. For example, you might get directions on how to do insurance coding (or some other job that's equally impossible to learn from the brief information they give you) plus a listing of all the doctor's offices in your area who use insurance coders.

What the packet does not tell you is that most of those offices have full-time employees whose job description includes insurance coding. It also does not tell you that you could have gotten the same contact information from the Yellow Pages for free. If 50,000 other people around the country were taken in by the same ad, the people who ran it have made $750,000. Not a bad moneymaker for them, but a terrible one for you.

If a job sounds too good to be true, it is. If it promises a lot of money with minimal training, plus the option of working from home or setting your own hours (and the ads don't usually say exactly what you will be doing), it's likely a scam. Lots of ads even say, "Tired of gimmicks and scams?"

It should never cost you money to apply for a job. If you come across job "opportunities" that make big promises while offering little information, run the other way.

Getting the Job

First off, if you happen to see a Help Wanted sign, make sure you look presentable before you ask for an application. Sometimes, the person taking the application will say, "Oh, the manager's right there. Let me get him for you." That will not be good if you have half-purple hair, a stained shirt, and body odor (unless you are applying at a shop where this is the dress code). You do not need to dress up to pick up an application, but make sure that you are at least clean and neat.

Write neatly on the application. Most of the time, the application will ask for references. This is where your coaching team comes in handy. Use them for references, and if you have any reference letters from teachers or past bosses, including people you've babysat for or done yardwork for or whatever, attach them to the application.

Sometimes, someone might interview you right when you turn in an application. Other times, you'll get a phone call when they are ready to interview people. Either way, follow these simple tips to make a good impression:

- Dress neatly and cleanly.
- Shake hands when the interviewer introduces himself or herself to you.
- Talk respectfully. Avoid cussing and a lot of slang. In other words, use adult-speak.
- Be honest. Do not lie about your job experience or about anything else that your interviewer asks you.
- Do not ramble. If, like me, you chatter when you're nervous, practice interviewing with a friend beforehand.
- Take time to think about your answer. When the interviewer asks a question that requires more than a yes or no answer, take a moment to think before you start talking. This will help you avoid rambling.
- Shake hands again as you leave, and thank the interviewer for his or her time.

The Humiliation

Nothing is as much fun as someone coming in and seeing you at your wonderful new job and laughing, "Hey, good move. Left home so that you could be a big success at McDonald's! Ha, ha, ha!"

I'll give you the same advice that your mom gave you about playground bullies: Ignore them.

Easier said than done, I know. But really, you don't have much choice. Just smile a fake grin and repeat one of these statements to yourself silently, over and over, until the annoying person leaves:

- I am doing this by choice.
- This is just step one of my plan.
- I will not be here forever.
- I am being responsible for my life.

Say whatever you need to say to yourself to keep from putting the jerk down and getting in trouble on the job. The bottom line is that you have a plan and this is part of it. Is it your favorite part? I doubt it, but it is a necessary part. So grit your teeth, do a good job, and soon you will move on to something else.

A great saying is, Living well is the best revenge. Think about that when you are really annoyed with or angry at other people. Is it fair that some people have easier lives, with great parents or inherited money or grandparents who give them cars? Of course not. But that's life. If some of those people don't understand the choices you are making or ridicule you for them, ignoring them is just the first step toward revenge.

The second, more important step, is building for yourself the life you want. In a few years, when you are barely in your 20s, you will be well on your way to the life you really want, and you will be accomplishing it on your own. In contrast, the idiot making fun of your job might still be relying on other people for everything in his or her life. Maybe he'll be stuck in some entry-level job for the rest of his life because he wasn't willing to really work, even at fast-food restaurants, for what he wanted. Or maybe he'll be making tons of money, but he'll be unhappy because he only became a lawyer, doctor, or whatever because his parents expected him to.

You, on the other hand, are making your own choices and finding your own way. That is something to be proud of, even if you find your short-term job to be a bit embarrassing.

Expert Advice: Tips for Teen Job Seekers

1. Consider what skills you want to develop in your next job. Do you want to become a better communicator? Lose your shyness? Become a better problem solver? Make the world a better place? A little thought goes a long way here.

2. Next, start networking. Ask around to see whether your teachers, coaches, neighbors, friends, or friends' parents know of a great work opportunity that fits your expectations.

3. It never hurts just to walk into the place you want to work (assuming it's a public place), smile big, and ask if they are accepting applications for employment. If so, ask who the manager is so that you can arrange a quick visit when you return with the completed application.

4. Don't be afraid to fill out more than one application, and don't be afraid of rejection. It usually takes up to 10 applications to get an offer, depending on your local job market.

5. When interviewing with a company, remember this: It is more important to be liked than to be right. In other words, don't stress out about your qualifications or having smart answers to every question. Just be polite, interested, and let your great personality shine through.

—*Tracy Laswell Williams, Executive Director,*
CAREER-Magic.com, and Author, *The Essential Job Search Companion*

By the Numbers

Average Hourly Pay for Typical Part-Time Teen Jobs

Kitchen workers $7.09

Waiters/Waitresses* . . . .$4.05 + tips

Retail—clothing shop $7.83

Child care worker $8.37

Clerical/Receptionist $8.81

Cashier $7.41

Sales counter clerk $6.75

Pizza delivery person** . . . .$9.00 + tips

Lifeguard** $8.00

* Waiters and waitresses do not have to be paid minimum wage because they earn tips. They must be paid at least $2.13 per hour, though. Wait staff in restaurants that serve alcohol usually must be at least 18 years old.

** These amounts estimated from online employment ads. All other amounts from the Bureau of Labor Statistics as of July 2002, http://stats.bls.gov/ncs/ocs/sp/ncbl0540.pdf.

Less Common Teen Jobs

Teen jobs are not limited to fast food, retail, and yard work. A quick, informal survey came up with the following and many other jobs for teens. What you pursue will depend in part on what you are familiar with, what you know how to do, and what you like to do.

- Assembly worker for a small company

- Assistant (to a photographer, writer, plumber, scientist, engineer)

- Auto parts driver

- Day care worker

- Garden helper/farm laborer

- Kennel care/animal care

- Marketer (approaching people in the mall to take a survey)

- Personal care assistant for someone with disabilities

- Ranch hand

- Reserve Officers Training Corps cadet (college students only)

- Swimming pool cleaner

- Temporary agency worker

- Tutor

- Valet

- Web designer

- Also, paid internships are great if you can find one in the field you want to build a career in. Sometimes you can get school credit while you get paid. They are a foot in the door to your dream career.

How to Keep Your Job

Keeping your job is not that hard to do, but if you need reminders, here's what to do to keep yours:

- Show up! Call if you have to miss a day. Put your work schedule on your calendar so that you can keep track of it.
- Be honest. Do not take things that don't belong to you or try to sneak out of work early.
- Be realistic about how many hours you can work. It's better to say, "No, I'm sorry, but I'm not available to work on Sunday," than to agree to do it and then not show up because you are too tired.
- Stay off the phone. Leave your cell phone at home or in the car when you are working. Employers do not pay you to talk to your friends.
- Listen to your supervisor. Then follow the directions.

Creating a Resume

You probably do not actually need a resume for many of the jobs you will be applying for, but having one looks good, and in some cases, employers will let you hand in a resume instead of filling out an application, which is quite handy.

Resumes can be overwhelming because so many options for designing them exist, but it is really very simple. A resume is just a professional-looking list of your educational and job information, plus any specific skills or qualifications you have.

For a simple resume, just follow the format in the sample resume. It will work even if you have no job experience in the area in which you are looking for a job. You can certainly get fancier than this, but make sure you include the basics: what kind of job you want, how much schooling you have, what job experiences you have, what related skills you have, and who can vouch for you. This is information employers must have about you.

Plenty of software programs, including common word processing programs like Microsoft Word and Word Perfect, allow you to simply plug in your information to create a resume. You can also get a book from the library or look at resume forms online. The key, at this point, is just to keep it simple.

Long-Term Career Plans

So, you have accepted the fact that you are not going to get your dream job right away. However, maybe you have another problem entirely—maybe you don't even know what your dream job is.

Career planning can be an overwhelming decision, and several theories on the best way to do it exist. One common method to determine a career goal is to take some kind of vocational test. These tests ask you lots of questions about your interests, your skills, the kind of atmosphere you like, your personality, and so on. The results give you a list of careers for which you are well suited.

One common vocational inventory is the Armed Services Vocational Aptitude Battery (ASVAB), which is administered by the U.S. military at thousands of high schools across the country. This three-hour test is part of the ASVAB Career Exploration Program. Your local armed forces recruiter can also give it. If you meet other recruitment criteria and are interested in a career in the military, your local recruiter can administer the test. Some recruiters will administer the test to anybody who is interested, even if you are not joining the military. Check with your local recruiter to find out his or her policy. To find your local recruiter, check online at http://www.todaysmilitary.com/ns/t5_ns_recruiting.php or look in your phone book in the blue government pages. Check under recruiting in the U.S. Government section.

Your school guidance counselor can help you find local vocational testing, and if you try that, perhaps one of the careers will be something that makes you think, "Aha! That sounds great. It would be perfect for me!"

If so, wonderful.

But what if your vocational testing says that you would make a terrific accountant, and the idea bores you stiff? Well, then, you ignore it. You certainly don't want to spend your life doing something that bores you, right?

Barbara Sher has another approach, one I really like. In her book *I Could Do Anything, If I Only Knew What It Was* (1995), Sher says that we should not choose our career based just on what we are good at.

Sample Resume

Cindy Bitford
1034 Aloma Avenue
Winter Park, FL 32789
407/699-3040
cindyb@msn.com

> Make sure your employer can reach you

GOAL: A job of 30 + hours per week where I can use my clerical skills

EDUCATION: Winter Park High School
Will graduate in June 2007

> If you have had several jobs, list them in order from most recent to least recent. However, make sure your resume is only one page long. If you have too many jobs to fit on one page, leave out the ones least related to the job you are trying to get.

EXPERIENCE: April 2002–Present
Child Care Provider
The Barnes Family
Winter Park, Florida
Duties include taking care of children and cooking

AREAS OF KNOWLEDGE: Type 80 words per minute, strong grammar and punctuation skills, excellent spelling, good computer skills. National Honor Society member. Interest in wild animals, pets, biology.

REFERENCES: John and Carrie Barnes
407/328-8888

Dr. Robert Hans (Guidance Counselor)
Winter Park High School
407/356-4000

Elizabeth Bell (English Teacher)
Winter Park High School
407/312-8512

> This would be a good list of knowledge areas for a resume for a job at the zoo. If you were applying at a car repair shop, emphasize knowledge related to cars.

> Make sure you ask before listing people as references. If possible, get a letter of reference from each person and attach copies of them to your resume.

Thank goodness, I am an excellent typist. Do I want to type for a living? No way. Although, come to think of it, I do a lot of typing in my career as a writer.

Sher (1995) recommends asking yourself what you love doing. What do you enjoy so much that you would pay to do it? What makes you feel connected to the world and to other people? What makes you happy? Now, take those answers and think about what career you can build around that activity.

Do you absolutely love working with little kids? Then some of your options include teacher, camp counselor, child psychologist, interior designer specializing in kids' rooms, party planner, children's entertainer, tutor, day care worker, and retail sales in a children's store. And those are just some of the options!

What if you dream of being a singer, but your voice is not very good? Well, have you taken lessons? Have you really, truly practiced and devoted time and effort to improving your voice? If you have, and it still stinks, then it is fine to face reality. But that does not mean singing cannot figure into your dream career. Maybe you will be a voiceover actor, a karaoke bar owner, a talent scout for a record label, a director of stage musicals, or a musician with some instrument other than your voice.

Sher's (1995) point is that you cannot ignore your dreams. You need to find meaningful work for your life. That is the work that will pay your bills (although not necessarily make you rich), keep you connected, and make you happy.

I like this philosophy because, let's face it, we are all good at something we don't like. Maybe it's playing piano or trimming hedges or doing backbends. But if it does not make us happy, why on earth would we want to build a career around that skill?

You can always bring your dream job back to your short-term job and connect them. Let's say your singing stinks, despite your best efforts for several years, but you have decided to pursue a career in the music industry, possibly as a sound engineer. Now you need a job while you finish high school before entering a vocational-technical school (one that emphasizes practical job skills) with a program in sound engineering.

You could just take any part-time job and look at it as a step along the way, because it is allowing you to finish high school and then move on to the program you want. Or, you might try to find a job that is actually related to your chosen field. As a high school student, some options you might look into are:

- a clerical job at a local music production company;
- an internship at the community access channel, to learn a bit about sound engineering and the equipment used;
- a job doing anything at the vocational-technical school that offers the program, which will give you the opportunity to meet others pursuing the same goal, talk to some of the teachers, and maybe even sit in on a class to see if you really like it;
- a disc jockey job; or
- a job as an assistant to the sound person at a local theater.

The point is that if you can get a job that is in some small way connected to your eventual goal, that job will feel more purposeful and more rewarding. If you cannot get a job that's somehow connected, you just need to remind yourself regularly what you are working toward. Keep looking for opportunities to hook up with other folks pursuing that same dream. That way you can start to learn more about it and get a clearer feel for the coursework and the actual job itself.

You could also follow the work-itself-out theory. In that theory, you start college, declare a major that you know you will change sooner or later, and just start taking your basic classes. Then, you hope that you will find a calling while you are in college so that you can earn a degree that will actually be useful in your career. Now, nothing is really wrong with that approach, and it works for many people, but it can be hard to make all the sacrifices you will need to make to attend college when you don't even know why you are going.

Your career goals may change. In fact, they almost certainly will. But if you are entering college with absolutely no idea of what you want to do with your life, make sure you stick to the basic courses and give your career a lot of thought. You don't want to struggle through two years of biology and anatomy for pre-medicine only to decide that you really want to be a fabric artist. It will not be the end of your life if you do, but why spend the time and money if you don't have to?

Resources

Books

Bolles, R. N. (2004). *What color is your parachute?* Berkeley, CA: Ten Speed Press.

Editors of VGM Career Books. (2000). *Resumes for first-time job hunters*. Chicago: McGraw-Hill/Contemporary Books.

Edwards, P., & Edwards, S. (1996). *Finding your perfect work*. New York: G.P. Putnam's Sons.

Fry, R. W. (2001). *Your first resume: For students and anyone preparing to enter today's tough job market*. Franklin Lakes, NJ: Career Press.

Kise, J. A. G., & Stark, D. (1996). *LifeKeys*. Minneapolis, MN: Bethany House.

McNeill, W. (2000). *First time resume*. Avon, MA: Adams Media Corporation.

Murphy, J. T. (2001). *Success without a college degree*. Seattle, WA: Achievement Dynamics.

Sher, B. (1994). *I could do anything, if I only knew what it was*. New York: Delacorte Press.

Websites

About.com
http://careerplanning.about.com/library/weekly/aa051799.htm
This site offers information on the career planning process.

The Career Key
http://www.careerkey.org/english/
Take an online career test and learn more about jobs that might interest you.

Career Magic
http://www.CAREER-Magic.com
Lots of good articles on job hunting, plus you can e-mail in your career and job hunting questions.

Job Corps
http://jobcorps.doleta.gov/
Job Corps is a government program offering education, a place to live, and job training to kids 16 and older who are economically disadvantaged and are either high school dropouts or are in need or more job training. You can also reach Job Corps at 202/693-3900.

O*NET™ OnLine!
http://online.onetcenter.org/
This site makes occupational information interactive and accessible for all.

Quintessential Careers

http://www.quintcareers.com/teen_jobs.html

This site offers job and career resources for teenagers.

U.S. Department of Labor

http://www.doleta.gov/youth_services/yocorner/job/checklist.cfm

Help on finding a job, from the U.S. Department of Labor

U.S. Department of Labor, Bureau of Labor Statistics

http://www.bls.gov/oco/home.htm

The Occupational Outlook Handbook

CHAPTER 6

The Home Team
Finding a Place to Live

Before you start looking for a place to live, take a few minutes to think about what you need. Maybe you dream of having a cool apartment with retro furniture in an apartment complex with a swimming pool and game room.

Welcome to real life. Your first apartment is probably not going to be all that cool. I don't say that to discourage you, I just want you to focus on the really important stuff for now. And what is important? Well, you need to be safe. You need an apartment that is close to work and school, and you need a place you can afford.

If it makes you feel better, start a notebook or folder and fill it with pictures and ideas of all the neat things you will have in your home someday, but don't focus on them now. Right now, independence is your number one priority, even if it means living in a dump for a while. If you are not willing to do that, you probably don't want independence enough to get it.

Remember, even if your new place is kind of gross, it will be *your* place. A place where you will have privacy. A place where your friends will be welcome. A place where you are in charge.

Your Options

I've been saying apartment, but apartments aren't your only option, of course. The following is a rundown of the most common housing arrangements for teens.

- **Apartment**. An apartment in an apartment building is an individual unit with its own bedroom, bathroom, and kitchen. One building has lots of units. Sometimes the landlord pays for utilities, but sometimes each tenant (that's you) pays for his or her own utilities. Some apartment complexes have nice extras like pools, community rooms, and tennis courts. A studio apartment (also called an efficiency), the cheapest kind, is really just one big living room/ sleeping area. The only closed-off part of a studio apartment is the bathroom.

You often must sign a one-year lease to rent an apartment, so make sure you choose a good one. You will have to pay a security deposit before moving in, which

Definitions

Utilities: Utilities are the services outside companies provide that are usually paid for on a monthly basis. Common utilities include electricity, gas, water, sewer, and garbage removal. In apartment buildings and dorm rooms, you often only have to pay for electricity and gas.

is usually one month's rent that you pay in addition to your first month's rent. You will not get the security deposit back if you move out early or if you trash the apartment.

- **Dorm Room.** A dorm room is a room inside a dormitory building or residence hall on a school campus or within walking distance of it. Each bedroom usually has two or three people sharing it, although some schools have single rooms available, too. Dorm rooms are usually furnished, and each cluster of bedrooms might have a living room to share as well. Most colleges and universities have dormitories, but they often have waiting lists. You must be a student actively enrolled in the school to live in a dorm room. Usually, students in each cluster or suite share a large bathroom. Many dorms have no cooking facilities, and students are required to purchase meal plans from the college cafeteria. Some dorms have apartment-style dorms, including kitchens. Dorms are often single-gender, for either guys or girls. Students do not pay utility costs at most dorms. Those are included in the "rent." Cable TV, Internet connections, and telephone lines are sometimes included. You usually rent a dorm room for one semester at a time. Dorm rooms average about $1,700 to more than $5,000 per semester.
- **Friend or Relative's House.** This is when you stay with a friend or relative, obviously. You might have your own bedroom or you might need to share with your friend. You will share the bathroom and kitchen with everyone who lives in the house or apartment. These arrangements vary. Your friend or his or her parents might let you stay free for a little while as you save up money, but this is generally a short-term deal to help you get on your feet. If you are staying with a friend for the long-term, you are a roommate, and you need to work out the details on rent, utilities, and so forth.
- **Boarding Rooms.** These are not that common, but they do still exist, especially in some college towns. Boarding is when you rent a bedroom in a person's house. Sometimes, your rent includes some meals. Boarding almost always includes kitchen privileges. You will need to share the bathroom with everyone else in the house. Utilities are usually included in this arrangement. This option does not give you much privacy, but it is usually much cheaper than renting your own apartment. If you don't plan to be home much because of work and school, it might work out well for you.

Expert Advice: Finding a Home

Before you start looking, make sure that you are legally allowed to sign a lease. State laws vary, but in many states, a person younger than 18 can legally enter into a contract if it is for necessary things like food and shelter. Call your state's family court or legal aid office to find out the laws in your area.

Check out the management. Walk through the complex and see how it is maintained. Do the buildings and grounds appear to be in good repair? Knock on a few doors and ask people who live there if they are happy with the apartment and the landlord. If nobody wants to talk to you, that's a bad sign.

Call the Better Business Bureau to check on complaints against the apartment complex. Check with small claims court to see how many times the landlord has been sued for not returning security deposits. Make sure you will get a receipt every month for your rent payment. Ask if an on-site manager, maintenance person, or phone number to call is available in emergencies that will get you a prompt response. There should be.

Don't Forget:

- Visit during rush hour. Check traffic tie-ups and traffic noise.
- If your unit is near the pool, count on it being much noisier during the summer.
- Are there noise-producing things nearby (i.e., trains, factories, airports)? Ask other tenants about them.
- If your unit is next to the community room or the laundry room, go by at night to check out the noise.
- Call the police department to check on number of crimes (i.e., burglaries, car thefts, etc.) for that neighborhood.

The Lease:

- If the landlord tries to pressure you into signing a lease immediately, walk away. That's the right decision 9 out of 10 times.
- Any lease that shifts the management burden (fixing the plumbing, heating, etc.) to the tenant is bad news. If your ceiling is leaking, it is the landlord's job to fix it.
- The lease should include everything that the landlord has promised you. If the lease says no pets, and the manager says that your small dog is allowed, write that on the lease and have the manager sign and date the note.

Before You Move in:

- Walk through the apartment with the property manager or leasing agent and document all pre-existing damage (stains on carpet, dented door, faded blinds, etc.). Make a list and have the leasing agent or property manager sign and date it. This will help protect your security deposit by proving that you did not inflict the damage.
- Start a file to keep track of your rental credit. Keep a copy of the lease, your monthly rent receipts, your paid utility bills, and so on. This will help establish good credit for the next home you move into, so that you don't have to be treated like a first-time renter a second time.

—Attorney Steven R. Kellman, Director of the Tenants Legal Center of San Diego, www.tenantslegalcenter.com

Housing Discrimination

If you suspect that someone has denied you housing because of your race, gender, marital status, religion, age, disability, or national origin, or because you have a child, stand up and make yourself heard! Any time you feel you may have been discriminated against, report it to your local fair housing office, legal aid office, or the Department of Housing and Urban Development. They can send "testers" to that complex to see if you are being treated wrongfully. You might choose not to live there anyway because of their attitude, but reporting the discrimination is the best way to protect your rights and hopefully put a stop to such illegal practices.

—Attorney Steven R. Kellman
Director of the Tenants Legal Center of San Diego
www.tenantslegalcenter.com

Searching for a Place

Before you can start your home hunt, it is important to figure out what you must have in an apartment (again, I am using the term apartment, but I mean any of the options discussed previously).

If you have a pet (my cat lived with me in at least 10 different apartments throughout college), then you can cross all no-pets options off your list.

If you do not have a car, then you need to find a place close to school and work or on the bus, subway, or train route.

If you want to live alone, you will likely only be able to afford an efficiency or studio apartment. If you want lots of company, you might look for a group of people living in a 3- or 4-bedroom place who need a new roomie.

Take a few minutes to write down what you absolutely must have in an apartment. These will be deal breakers, the things that will keep you from even looking at a place if it does not offer them.

When I moved out of the house, I had a cat, a washer, and a dryer. So, my deal breakers were that a place had to allow pets and had to have a washer and dryer hookup. I also hate driving in heavy traffic (and Orlando always has heavy traffic!), so I wanted someplace close to school and my various jobs. So, I started out looking at places very close to the University of Central Florida. From that list, I narrowed it down by crossing off places that did not allow pets and had no washer and dryer hookup.

Where to Look

You have lots of ways to look for apartments. If you have narrowed the boundaries of where you want to live, you can just drive around and see them. Most cities also have apartment directories, often at the entryway to grocery stores and libraries. These directories are free, and they have listings and advertisements for all the major apartment complexes. The cheapest appartments may not be listed, though.

You can also go to an apartment search service, where a person will help you narrow down your list and will direct you to apartments that meet your criteria. You don't pay for these services: Apartments pay fees to be on their list of possibilities. Small apartment complexes may be left out of this search.

Interpreting Classified Ads

Looking through the classified ads is a great way to find a new home, but you might think the ads are written in a different language. Here are some common abbreviations.

2/1 or 1/1 . . . . .two bedrooms/one bath, one bedroom/one bath

a/c . . . . .air conditioning

ba, bth . . . . .bath

bd, bdrm . . . . .bedroom

cbl . . . . .cable

dw . . . . .dishwasher

eff or stu . . . . .efficiency or studio

gar . . . . .garage

mo . . . . .month

osp . . . . .off-street parking

(they have a parking lot or garage for tenants)

pkg . . . . .parking

sec dep . . . . .security deposit

sep ent . . . . .separate entrance

(you do not have to walk through
the rest of the house to enter your room)

util . . . . .utilities

w/d . . . . .washer/dryer

Driving around is the best way to find a small apartment or a boarding room. Often, just as the fall semester gets going, signs will crop up saying "Room for rent" on front lawns, and vacancy signs show up on small apartment complexes. In some cities, housing goes fast, and you might have to wait several months for an available unit. Start looking early.

For dormitory information, you should contact the housing department at the college or university you are attending.

The Internet is a great resource for apartment hunting. Several sites, like Homestore.com's http://www.springstreet.com/apartments/home.jhtml?gate=rnet, let you search for an apartment in your town or across the country. You can specify price range, number of bedrooms, and so on. Also, many major newspapers have their classified ads online, so you can narrow down your search by computer.

What to Ask the Landlord

If you've never looked for an apartment before, you might not know what to ask. You look at the apartment, it looks good, that's it. Right? Wrong. Renting an apartment or becoming roommates with someone else who rents an apartment is a big commitment. Make several copies of Worksheet 4 and fill it out as you look at various apartments, dorm rooms, and so on. Here are some things you need to find out and put on the worksheet:

- Monthly rent
- Date due
- Penalties for late rent
- Security deposit
- Date available
- Number of bedrooms
- Number of bathrooms
- Whether uilities are included
- Cooking options
- Laundry facilities
- Length of lease
- Penalty for breaking the lease
- If having roommates is okay
- Whether there is a security system
- Age of building
- Who does maintenance and repairs
- Whether you can paint or decorate
- If pets are allowed
- Rules on overnight guests
- Whether an office or apartment manager is on-site
- Who to contact for emergency repairs

Definitions

Lease: This is a legal agreement that you sign, so make sure you actually understand it. Some things the lease will cover are who is living in the apartment (and it should include everybody living there), how much the rent is, when the rent is due, what the penalty is for late payment, how long the lease period is, what happens if you move out before the lease period is up, how much the security deposit is, under what conditions will you get your security deposit returned, and whether pets are allowed.

How to Find a Roommate

Plenty of ways to hook up with roommates exist, but your first step is to figure out what you want from a roommate. Do you like to be social, throw parties, and have friends over a lot? Or do you want quiet when you come home so you can relax or study? Do you care if your roommate smokes? Do you definitely want your own bedroom, or are you willing to share? Are overnight guests (of either gender) an issue? Do you want to share cooking responsibilities, or will you each be on your own?

Think about these questions. Brainstorm about the perfect roommate! Then, make a list of qualities you would like your roommate to have (neat, cooks, allows pets) or that you definitely do not want him or her to have (smokes, wants everything quiet).

With this list, you are ready to hunt. Here are some places to find roommates:
- newspaper (city or school) classified ads;
- bulletin boards at libraries, grocery stores, or on campus;
- word of mouth (tell everyone you know you are looking for a roommate); and
- coworkers.

Keep in mind, if you are answering someone else's ad for a roommate, you will need to make sure not only that you get along with them, but also that the apartment meets all your criteria regarding cost, location, and so forth.

Try to meet at least four or five people before you decide on a roommate. Be polite, but be very honest about what you are looking for in a roommate. You might like someone as a person, but that doesn't mean you can live together. Generally, people with similar social habits, priorities, and budgets make the best roommates.

Before you move in together, draw up a roommate agreement. Spell it out so no one will have misunderstandings. Who gets which bedroom? Can visitors spend the night? Who is going to clean the bathroom, and how often? Write it down now to avoid

Worksheet 4

Home-Hunting

Apartment	Address	Contact	Phone	Rent	Sec. Dep.	Bedrooms	Baths	Kitchen	Pets	Date Avail.	Utilities	Notes

problems later. For online samples of roommate agreements, see the resources section at the end of this chapter.

How to Keep a Roommate

Talk to each other! Biting your tongue will lead to resentment. If it really bothers you that your roommate forgets to pass along your phone messages, talk to him or her about it! Then put a pad of paper and a pen by the phone to help him or her remember. Talking, then action, will solve most of your problems.

Do what you say you will do. If you are supposed to clean the bathroom on Saturdays, it's that simple. You're independent now, and you have got to keep up with your responsibilities.

Don't expect your roommate to be your best friend. If he or she becomes a buddy, great, but living together does not obligate that person to listen to you whine or vent or to help solve your problems. Also, you should not get sucked into trying to solve someone else's problems. Some of the strongest roommate relationships grow between people who live completely separate lives but like the same kind of home atmosphere.

Be willing to give in. You've realized by now that independence doesn't mean you get your own way all the time, right? If you share an apartment, you will be doing a lot of compromising. When you and your roommate disagree, talk about the options and try to find a middle ground where you both give in a little bit.

Renter's Insurance

What is it? Renter's insurance is insurance that covers your belongings in case your apartment or dorm room is burglarized or lightning knocks out your television, or whatever. It also covers items stolen out of your car and is pretty inexpensive.

Let's say you have renter's insurance and your roommate's ex-boyfriend steals your computer and stereo. Your insurance will cover your losses after you pay your deductible of $100 (or whatever deductible your policy has).

Renter's insurance costs $10 to $30 per month. You may never use it, but if you have stuff you couldn't afford to replace (and don't we all), it's a bargain. You might never need it, but if you do, you'll really need it.

Resources

Books

Burkett, L., & Strauss, E. (2000). *Renting your first apartment*. Chicago: Moody Press.

Gilchrist, P. (2002). *Decorating your first apartment*. Asheville, NC: Lark Books.

Hanson, J. (2002). *The real freshman handbook: A totally honest guide to life on campus*. Boston: Houghton-Mifflin.

Portman, J., & Stewart, M. (2002). *Renters' rights: The basics* (3rd ed.). Berkeley, CA: Nolo Press.

Websites

To find information about the laws about renting specific to your state, go to a search engine and type in "tenants' rights" and your state. For example, type "tenants' rights Oregon" in the search window at Yahoo or Google or your search engine to find a website with more details.

About.com

> http://apartments.about.com/library/articles/bl_abbreviations.htm
> This includes a list of more classified advertisement abbreviations.
> http://apartments.about.com/library/weekly/aa080601b.htm
> The rental agreement and roommates.

Insure.com

> http://www.insure.com/home/renters.html
> This site includes renter's insurance information.

iStudentCity.com

> http://www.istudentcity.com/housing/housing_longterm_dorm.asp
> This includes information about dorm rooms.

National Accessible Apartment Clearinghouse

> http://www.forrent.com/naac/
> Find an apartment designed for special needs.

NOLO Law for All

> http://www.nolo.com/lawcenter/
> This site has roommate agreement samples and other tenant information.

Tenants Legal Center of San Diego

> www.tenantslegalcenter.com
> Although this information is based on California law, it includes lot of good general information.

CHAPTER 7

A Ride to the Pool
The Basics of Transportation

hink of some of the great road trip movies: *Boys on the Side*, *Crossroads*, and *Thelma and Louise*. These movies show how we associate independence with the open road. A car and a highway represent the freedom to go wherever you choose. That is why from about the age of 12, when we get tired of being dropped off at the movies, we're wishing for our own set of wheels. With a car and a tank full of gas, you can go any direction you want.

Of course, cars are not always a good thing. Think *Maximum Overdrive*, *Jeepers Creepers*, *Rat Race*, *Changing Lanes*...Watch a couple of these and you will realize a car is not always the answer to your problems.

Still, one thing is certain. You are going to have to find a way to get around.

Where Do You Need to Go?

What kind of transportation you will use affects many things. It can be a huge part of your budget, for instance. Or, if you will be riding a bus, the bus routes will determine where you can live and which jobs you can take.

The first thing to think about is where you need to go and how often you need to get there. Start with work, home, and school. Do you already have a good job that you want to keep? How close is it to where you will live? How many days a week will you work? Is your job along a bus or subway route?

What about grocery shopping? Friends to visit? A mall? The movie theater? The doctor's office? Jot down a list of all the places you go occasionally, even if you do not go to them every week.

Buy or print out a map of your town or city. On the map, mark all the places you go regularly. Now look at it. Are your marks clustered fairly close together? Great, your transportation question just got easier. If they are spread from one end of the map to the other, however, unless your city has an excellent mass transit system, your budget just got tighter.

Your Options

You have five basic transportation options, each with their own pros and cons:

- **Walking.** Walking (or skating, blading, or scootering) is only realistic as your main mode of transportation if you live in a very small town or if you live, work, and go to school all in a small area, like on a college campus. Walking is free and it is good for you, two big pluses. On the minus side, walking takes a lot of time, and bad weather can be a real pain. Also, walking at night presents dangers in many areas. If you walk somewhere, however, you might be able to catch a ride home.

- **Biking.** Biking is still very low-tech. It's cheap and good exercise, too. It is faster than walking, but still not very realistic if you have to travel farther than a few miles more than twice a day. Bad weather and unsafe road conditions are hazards for cyclists, and if someone offers you a ride home, you have to figure out what to do with your bike.

- **Moped.** Mopeds are like miniature motorcycles, usually with engine displacement rates of 50 ccs or less and top speeds of 30 to 40 miles per hour. Each state has its own criteria for when a moped becomes a motorcycle. Check this out with your state's department of motor vehicles. Your vehicle's classification will determine what kind of licensing you need, how much insurance you need, where you can ride it, where you can park, and more. You can get a new or pretty good used moped for $800 to $1,500. They get great gas mileage (often around 80 miles per gallon, compared to 20–25 miles per gallon for most cars). They are fairly low maintenance and are terrific for getting around campus or small towns. On the down side, you do need a driver's license and insurance, which increases the cost of this method of transportation. Mopeds are not safe (and may not be legal) on highways or chaotic big-city streets. Suburbs, small towns, and some college campuses are ideal for mopeds.

- **Mass Transit.** Mass transit is transportation run by large cities. It may consist of buses, trains, subways, or some combination of all three. If you live in a city big enough to have a decent transit system, use it! It's usually fairly cheap, and you don't have to buy any equipment, worry about maintenance, or pay for insurance. You can sleep, read, or do homework while you are riding. And, this is a safe option if you've been drinking or you are just plain exhausted, or both. The problems with mass transit are that you have to follow the schedule of the transit company, so you may end up arriving early or staying late at some places. Big-city buses, trains, or subways can be scary at night, depending on the crowd, so it is good to ride with someone, if possible. You also might have to walk several blocks from your home, school, or work to the nearest stop. The schedules can be confusing if you've never used them before, but after a month or two, you'll be a pro. Although you follow a schedule, this really gives you the most freedom in a big city. Mass transit means no parking hassles and is so much cheaper than a car.

- **Car.** This is what everyone typically wants, and depending on your situation, you may truly need one. The biggest appeal of a car is freedom. You go where you want, when you want. If you are used to strict rules and little personal freedom, a car can seem like the ticket to heaven. But a car has many, many disadvantages.

First of all, it's expensive. The car itself; the insurance rates, which are outrageously high for teen drivers; the oil changes and tune-ups—the list never seems to end. Oh, don't forget parking fees and gasoline costs, which keep rising by the day. In addition, buying a car requires careful research and shopping to make sure you get a good deal. Also, if you are the only person with a car in your circle of friends, you might be the go-to person for rides, which can get old fast. Basically, a car is a huge responsibility. If you feel your life is already full and that being independent is going to be overwhelming (and it will, at times), try to do without a car unless you absolutely must have one.

By the Numbers

Average Transportation Costs Per Year

During 1998, people younger than 25 spent an average of $2,084 toward the actual purchase of a car, $654 on gasoline and oil, $211 on finance charges, $357 on maintenance and repairs, and $383 on insurance, which is an average of $3,689 to drive and pay toward a car in one year. Unless they bought a cheap enough car that they paid it off within one year, they will continue paying that much in future years. And that's assuming you buy an inexpensive used car.

Compare that with about $1,000 for a good used moped, plus another few hundred for gasoline and insurance; $500 for a decent bike, helmet, and lock (375,000 bikes were stolen in the United States in 1998); $235 for an average year's worth of mass transit; $150 for good in-line skates; or $100 for nice walking shoes.

(All figures are from the *2000 Statistical Abstracts of the United States,* U.S. Bureau of the Census.)

Cars

Here's my last attempt to talk you out of buying a car!

Owning a car definitely has a plus side: No other mode of transportation gives you as much freedom. Freedom to go anywhere, to take friends along, to come and go on your own schedule…

But all that freedom comes at a high cost. The average new domestic car cost $18,725 in 1999, and the average new import cost $30,350 *(2000 Statistical Abstracts of the United States)*. This is not the kind of money that most newly independent teens have to spend.

Even a decent used car will set you back several thousand bucks, at least. Other expenses, as I already mentioned, include oil changes, tune-ups, insurance, parking, gasoline, and repairs. The expenses are not only in dollars. It takes time to shop for a car, compare insurance prices, and take it in for those oil changes and tune-ups. A car can gobble up your time and money, and you may not have much to spare of either one.

Another danger with a car is that you quickly become dependent on it. When you have access to a car, you choose jobs, schools, and homes that are not necessarily close to each other, because you have a car to get from place to place. Then, if your car conks out before you have paid it off, you have a lifestyle that requires a car, and you have car payments, but no car. Then you are looking at a second set of car payments while you're still paying for that first car that no longer runs.

If you really must have a car, my best advice is to save up and pay cash for one. It may not be hot. It might even be a 10-year-old carrot-colored Celica, as one of my first cars was. But if it is at a price you can afford, and if a trusted mechanic says it still has a few good years left on it, it's just the right fit for you. Remember, you want to control the car, you don't want the car to control you. If you get in over your head with an expensive car and car payments, you will find yourself arranging your life around making those car payments, and the bottom line is, a car is just a way to get from one place to another.

Car Shopping

Getting a good deal on a great car is a lot of work, and I will just cover the basics here to start you on your way. Make sure you have an adult with car-buying experience help you out here. This is one area where mistakes or poor judgment will cost you lots of hard-earned cash.

- Figure out your budget.
- Read through some car sales magazines and classified ads and see which cars fit your budget.
- Do some research. Look up reviews of particular models on websites like http://www.automobilereviews.com/, http://www.auto-reviews.com/, and http://www.edmunds.com/.
- Come up with three cars that would meet your needs and your budget, and begin shopping.
- Decide whether you would rather shop at a dealership or buy from an individual. Individuals offer lower prices, but you cannot protect yourself from lemons and you have to handle all the paperwork.
- Before you look at cars, find out the Kelley Blue Book value of the models you are interested in. Aim to buy the car for a price somewhere between the trade-in value and the retail value. By researching online, you will find out the car's value in your area of the country. You can also get Blue Book information from the library and from most banks.
- Follow the advice at http://www.insidercarsecrets.com/buyingused.html. Get out and look at some cars. Test drive at least 10 cars. Do not make an offer or talk price unless you have already done price research for that particular model and year!
- Before you purchase the car, have your own mechanic (not one employed by the dealership or a friend of the seller!) check over the car thoroughly. You should be able to get this done for $30 to $100, depending on how thorough the inspection is. The more in depth the better, particularly if you are buying an older car with lots of miles on it. This inspection can end up saving you lots of money.

Can I Afford a Car?

There are two ways to afford a car. One is to save up the money and pay cash. This way, you will not have to deal with getting approved for financing or making monthly payments. Do you have the money saved up? Can you get by without a car while you save up the money for a year or more?

The second way to buy a car is to make a down payment and finance the rest. That means that if you have $1,500 saved and you choose a $4,000 car, you will pay $1,500 right away and finance the remaining $2,500. Your payments will depend on what the interest rate on your financing is. A rule of thumb is that your monthly payments should not exceed 15% of your take-home pay. For instance, if you make $1,000 per month, your car payment should not be more than $150.

If you have $1,500 to put down on a car and can afford $150 per month for a car payment, you could finance $2,500 for two years at 8% and have a monthly payment of $113.06. To figure out various payment plans, simply check with your bank or car financing company, or use any of a number of online calculators (Edmunds.com has a nice one at http://www.edmunds.com/apps/calc/CalculatorController?pmtcalAction = basic_calc&tid = edmunds.finance.landing.calculators..1.*). Interest rates vary depending on your bank or finance company, your down payment, your credit history, and the economy. The lower the interest rate, the less you will end up paying for your car.

Keep in mind, before you know whether you can afford a car, you need to know what your monthly income will be, as well as your basic monthly expenses. Don't buy a car and then try to make your budget work around it. Get your budget straight and then decide how much, if any, car you can afford.

By the Numbers

Car Maintenance Tips

Your owner's manual is the best place for information about your car's maintenance needs, however, the following is a very general list of basic maintenance tasks:

Inspect lights and check tire pressure . . . . .At least monthly

Change oil and filter and lubricate chassis . . . . .3,000–5,000 miles or 3–4 months

Inspect belts and hoses . . . . .3,000–5,000 miles or 3–4 months

Rotate tires and balance wheels . . . . .6,000 miles or every other oil change

Inspect brakes . . . . .6,000 miles or every other oil change

Replace air filter .12,000–24,000 miles or as indicated by inspection

Check air conditioning performance . . . . .Annually, usually in the spring

Replace fuel filter . . . . .24,000–100,000 miles

Service automatic transmission . . . . .24,000–100,000 miles

Check wheel alignment . . . . .12,000–24,000 miles or as indicated by tire wear

Flush and refill cooling system . . . . .40,000–100,000 miles

Replace belts and hoses . . . . .60,000–100,000 miles or 5–8 years

Replace engine timing belt . . . . .60,000–100,000 miles or 5–8 years (when equipped)

—From California State Automobile Association,
From the Car Care & Repair section at http://www.csaa.com/

If You Are in a Car Accident

- Make sure you and your passengers are okay. Call 911 if you need medical assistance.

- Move your car as far out of the way as possible, and turn on your hazard lights.

- Call the police, even for minor accidents—this is the law.

- Call your insurance agent.

- Exchange information with the other driver. Get his or her name, address, phone number, insurance company, policy number, license plate number, and make of car. Copy this information down from his or her driver's license and insurance card.

- Get names and phone numbers of witnesses.

- Be careful of what you say. Do not discuss whose fault the accident was, and stay calm.

- Consider keeping a disposable camera in your glove box so that you can take pictures of the damage to both vehicles.

Resources

Books

Bibbins, N. (2002). *Bikes, scooters, skates and boards*. North Adams, MA: Storey Books.

Burkett, L., & Strauss, E. (2000). *Buying your first car*. Chicago: Moody Press.

Burkett, L., & Strauss, E. (2002). *The world's easiest pocket guide to buying your first car*. Chicago: Northfield.

Consumer Reports used car buying guide 2003. (2003). Yonkers, NY: Consumer Reports Books.

Glowacz, D. (1997). *Urban bikers' tricks & tips: Low-tech & no-tech ways to find, ride, and keep a bicycle*. Chicago: Wordspace Press.

Kelley blue book used car guide July-December 2004: Private party, trade-in, retail values, 1989-2003 used car and truck. (2004). Irvine, CA: Kelley Blue Book Co.

Websites

Autobytel.com

http://www.autobytel.com/

This site has comprehensive information for buying, owning, and selling cars.

AutoSite.com

http://www.autosite.com/library/advocate/howtobuy.asp

How to buy a used car.

California State Automobile Association

http://www.csaa.com/home/

This is a great site with tips on shopping for and maintaining your car. Also check out http://www.aaa.com to find the webpage for your local AAA.

Consumer Reports

http://www.consumerreports.org/main/content/detail_auto.jsp?

Consumer Reports' used-car buying guide.

Edmunds.com

http://www.edmunds.com/

This excellent site will be very helpful in researching cars.

Kelley Blue Book

http://www.kbb.com/

This website is great for researching the costs of a particular model and year car based on whether you are buying from a dealer or an individual.

The Motley Fool

http://www.fool.com/car/Buyingacar.htm

The Motley Fool's guide to buying a car.

USAA Educational Foundation

http://www.usaaedfoundation.org/auto/index.asp

USAA Educational Foundation's information on buying a car.

CHAPTER 8

Don't Drown in Debt
Controlling Your Finances

*I*ndependence means different things to different people. Maybe you are looking for privacy, freedom from abuse, or just the ability to make your own decisions. No matter what you hope to get out of independence, you need one thing: money.

Living an independent life takes money, and lots of it. Earning it isn't the only problem: You also have to figure out how to spend it wisely to be able to afford the things you need and want most. You also need to figure out how to save it so you can meet your long-term goals, whether they are buying a car or taking a vacation. You need to know how to keep track of it, so you know exactly what you've got.

Your Assets

Your assets are what you are starting off with right now, as you plan your independence. If you have $3,000 in savings, that's $3,000 in assets. Assets are important because you will have lots of expenses, including possibly buying a car and paying a security deposit on an apartment, before you even begin your independent life.

Your Income

Your income is the amount of money that you receive on a regular basis. Your job will provide most of your income. Other sources of income might include some form of government aid, if you are receiving any social services or Social Security money for a deceased parent; parental support, if your parents are supporting you in your quest for independence; or college financial aid, such as student loans, grants, and so on.

To start figuring out how much money you can spend on things, you need to know how much money you will have coming in. If you already have a job, here's how to figure out your monthly income. Let's say you work 30 hours per week at $7.50 per hour. First, multiply 30 by $7.50, and you get $225. Then multiply that amount by 4, because each month has four weeks. For this job, $225 times 4 equals $900. That's your beginning monthly income: $900.

(Yes, I do realize that a year has 52 weeks, not 48 weeks. But believe me, those four extra weeks of pay will disappear quickly, even if they are not in your budget. I think it is better to base your monthly budget on your typical four monthly paychecks.)

If you have income from any other sources, add that in, too. Maybe you have a parent or an older sister or brother who is willing to give you $200 per month to help you achieve independence. If this is the case, ask questions to see if this is something you can count on for at least a year, or if it will just be a help-you-out-when-they-can kind of situation. If it will be a regular monthly gift, be very grateful and add that to your beginning monthly income, for a total of $1,100.

Where Will Your Money Go?

Ha! Where will your money *not* go? You will be surprised at how fast your income gets spent. Most teens live paycheck to paycheck. That means that if they miss one paycheck, they cannot afford to pay their bills. This is because teens haven't had a lot of time to build up savings accounts, and they mostly work jobs that do not offer vacation or sick time. With only limited monthly income, you will have to be very careful about how you spend your money.

Your biggest expenses will likely be rent, transportation, and food. You also might need to pay for utilities, schooling, clothing, and insurance, and, hopefully, have a bit left over for fun. It's also smart to start saving money right away, and we will talk more about that in a few minutes. Even if you have been paying for your own clothes and entertainment for a couple of years, being responsible for all of your expenses can be overwhelming, even terrifying.

A basic budget will help you stay on track. A budget is a plan of how much money you will make and how you will spend it. Try not to think of a budget as something that will control you and not let you spend any money. Really, a budget is just a tool that you will use to get the things you want.

Make a Monthly Budget

Just fill in the numbers on Worksheet 5, and you are on your way to creating a budget. Some numbers, like your rent and monthly car payment or bus pass, are fixed. Fixed means they stay the same from month to month. Others, like your grocery and electricity bills, are nonfixed and vary from month to month, and you have at least some control over them. The nonfixed amounts are the ones you can adjust to make your budget work. Copy Worksheet 5 several times, because it will probably take several tries to make your budget come out right. Remember that each adjustment requires a corresponding change in behavior, too. You cannot just write down less money for food without then spending less money at restaurants and the grocery store. When your budget is filled out are your budgeted expenses more or less than your total income? If they are lower, congratulations! If they are higher, and they almost always are, it is time to start cutting. You are already planning on spending more than you earn.

Each month, keep track of your expenses on paper or online (see the resources list at the end of this chapter). This worksheet is your budget plan. Make a copy and mark it February, or whatever next month is. Then keep track of how much you actually spend on each category. At the end of the month, add everything up again. Did you stay within your budget?

Over Budget?

Now you probably have a better idea of how much it is going to cost you to live on your own. And what if it's going to cost you too much? Here are some things to think about.

First, financial planners often recommend that housing should cost only one-quarter of your income, and no more than one-third. So, if your income is $1,100, your monthly rent should be between $275 and $363 (i.e., $1,100 X 0.25 and $1,100 X 0.33). That probably lets out the luxury apartment you were hoping for. Finding an affordable apartment or dorm room is your best first step to a successful budget.

Second, a car payment of $100 to $300 per month is going to take a huge bite out of your budget. Not buying a car is the second biggest way to lighten your budget load. Look at Chapter 7 to see if you have a reasonable alternative for getting around. Even putting it off for a year or so will help you get settled in. If you don't buy a car, you also can cross gasoline, car repairs, and car maintenance off your budget.

Third, eating out is expensive. Even cheap fast food adds up quickly. Many, many independent teens survive on sandwiches, ramen noodles, and the occasional cheap pizza. I'm not saying you should never eat out, but even 99-cent value items will eventually take their toll on your body and your budget. I'll share some budget-saving kitchen tips in Chapter 11.

Bank Accounts

To take care of all your financial transactions, you are going to need bank accounts. At the minimum, you will want to set up a checking and a savings account.

Worksheet 5

My Monthly Budget

Income
- Job _____
- Other _____
- Other _____
- **Total income** _____

Fixed Expenses
- Rent _____
- Car insurance _____
- Car payment _____
- Other Insurance _____
- **Total fixed expenses** _____

Variable Expenses
- Groceries _____
- Electricity _____
- Water _____
- Natural gas _____
- Trash removal _____
- Credit cards _____
- Long-term savings _____
- Short-term savings _____
- Gasoline _____
- Car repairs/maintenance _____
- Fun money _____
- Medical _____
- Gifts _____
- Haircuts/self-care _____
- Classes/activities _____
- Clothing _____
- **Total variable expenses** _____
- **+ Total fixed expenses** _____
- **= TOTAL EXPENSES** _____

Ten Ways to Cut Your Expenses

1. Buy used. Thrift stores are a great way to get clothes and household items without spending a lot of money.

2. Cook and freeze. Convenience foods (boxes of food that are prepackaged that you just heat up) are very expensive. Instead, cook one or two easy meals a week (like lasagna and tacos) and freeze them in individual serving sizes.

3. Turn off lights. Run the air a little higher or the heat a little lower. Ask for an energy audit and find out what you can do to lower your utility bills.

4. Go free. In big cities, many museums, zoos, and other attractions have free days once a month. Make a list of the things you would like to do, then call and find out if they have free or discounted times.

5. On the same note, find out cheap times. Some movie theaters offer cheaper-than-matinee rates from 4:00 p.m. to 5:30 p.m. Bowling is cheaper on weekdays. Restaurant lunches are less expensive and almost as big as dinners. You can still do some of the stuff you want to do, but try to figure out the cheapest way to do it.

6. Trade. Offer to babysit your nephew if your sister will sew you pillowcases like the ones you want from the home decorating stores. Help a friend paint his or her kitchen cabinets in exchange for free pizza. You may not have much money, but you have skills that you can use.

7. Take care of yourself. Staying healthy isn't just good for you, it's cheaper, too. Losing pay because you are out sick can ruin your budget, and doctor's and dentist's bills add up fast.

8. Be honest. If your friends are planning a night out that you cannot afford, say so. Either come up with a cheaper plan or simply say, "That's not in the budget this time. You guys have a good time, and next week we'll rent a movie, ok?"

9. Prioritize. It's hard to give up things you're used to—movies out, eating what you want, having the family car to drive—but you're making it on your own now. You need to decide what is most important to you, and make sure you include that in your life. Some of the littler stuff, though, you're just going to have to do without.

10. Be practical. If your uncle wants to buy you a birthday present, don't ask for leather car seat covers. Instead, ask for something that will relieve some of the pressure on your budget. It can still be something fun, like movie theater gift certificates, or, if your budget is in really poor shape, something totally, unavoidably practical—like groceries.

First, find some banks with branch offices close to where you need them: You want something that is convenient to your home, work, and school. You will also want access to ATMs (automatic teller machines), which almost every bank provides, although often with ridiculous fees. Also, if you are computer-savvy, you will probably want a bank that offers online banking, so that you can pay some of your bills and make transfers online. Last, never put your money in a bank that is not FDIC-insured (FDIC is short for Federal Deposit Insurance Corporation). FDIC-insured means your money is protected in case of theft, economic depression, and so on.

Once you have a small group of banks that meet those criteria, find out more information. Some things to ask include:

- What is the minimum balance I have to keep in this account? Minimum balance means you can't let the balance dip below that amount, whether it is $10 or $1,000, without getting charged a fine.
- Is there a per-check charge for checking accounts? That means that in addition to paying for your checks to be printed and paying the amount that the check is written for, you will also pay a certain fee for every single check you write. Per-check fees are most common with business accounts, but ask to be sure.
- Are there any other monthly fees associated with the account?
- Does the account pay any interest? For savings accounts especially, look for an account that pays you the highest interest rate available. That way, your money makes a little money.
- Does the bank offer overdraft protection, so that if you write a check and don't have enough money in your checking account to cover it, the bank will automatically transfer money from your savings account, so that the check doesn't bounce?
- What fees are associated with the ATM card? Most banks have their own ATMs available at no charge to you, but if you want to get cash at the gas station or movie theater instead of at the bank, you are fined a hefty charge. It's often $1 to $2.50 or more, both for your bank and the bank who owns the ATM you use, which can add up to $2 to $5 every time you take out money from any place other than the bank.
- Does the bank offer debit cards? A debit card is accepted almost everywhere credit cards are accepted, but it deducts the money from your account immediately. That means you cannot run up bills you can't afford to pay. Also, debit card transactions show up on your monthly bank statements, making them easier to track. Although you do not pay interest fees on debit card transactions, many institutions are now charging a transaction fee, often 25 cents, each time you enter your personal identification number and use your debit card. Also, debit cards do not offer the protection that credit cards do for telephone and Internet purchases. With credit cards, you can challenge a charge if you don't receive the goods or services you paid for, but with debit cards, the money has already left your account. Your only option is to try to get a refund from the company that sold you the item.
- Can the bank handle direct deposits? That means that if your employer also offers the service, your paycheck can be directly deposited into your bank account, ready for you to write checks from or withdraw in cash. It saves you a trip to the bank. You still get a paycheck stub at work that helps you track your pay, taxes, and so forth.

Once you find the bank with the right answers for you, ask a teller to help you open an account. Some states require that you be 18 years old to open a checking account. If this is true in your state and if you are not 18, ask to speak to a bank manager. Explain your situation briefly and honestly. If there isn't any adult who would be willing to cosign for an account with you, tell the manager that. Explain that you are living independently (or soon will be) and ask what your options are for banking. If you are polite and honest, somebody will help you work this out, although you might have to try a few banks.

You will also need a social security number to open an account. You probably already have a social security card, but make sure you actually take it with you to the bank. Otherwise, you usually should not carry it around with you.

Keeping Track of Your Checking Account

Every time you write a check, write down the date, check number, who the check is made out to, and the amount of the check in your checkbook register. That's the little separate booklet with lots of lines for you to keep track of your checks.

I like duplicate checks. Those are checks that come with the real check plus a carbon copy behind each check. So when I write a check and hand it to the cashier, I'm left with a carbon copy showing me everything I need to know. Then, every day or every week—if I'm not writing many checks—I transfer all the checks written during that period into my register. I find out what my checking account balance is and subtract all the check amounts to figure out how much money is left in my account. Then I rip up the carbon copies and throw them away, unless I think I might need them to prove I made a certain purchase or paid a certain bill.

If you do not use duplicate checks, you need to write down the pertinent information in your checkbook register *right after you make out the check*. That's important. Don't wait until later, figuring that you will remember. It's incredibly frustrating to sit and try to recreate the past few days and figure out where you wrote checks and how much they were for. Believe me, I know.

Make sure to record withdrawals, deposits, and ATM and debit card transactions in your register as well. I like to write a little "C" on each receipt as I enter it in the checkbook register to help me remember that I already entered it. Don't throw those receipts away, however, until you balance your checkbook.

Balancing Your Checkbook

Each month, your bank will send you a statement. This is basically a list of all the activity on your account in the previous month. It will include all the checks that have been processed, deposits and withdrawals you have made, and other activity.

Make sure that you have updated your register and that you have added and subtracted up to the very last entry. Then lay out your receipts, your checkbook register, and your statement. Go through your checkbook and find each transaction that is listed on your statement. Check it off in your checkbook register (in the column with a checkmark at the top) and then cross it out or check it off on your statement.

If an amount is different in the check register and on the statement for an ATM transaction, deposit, or withdrawal, pull out the receipt to double-check it. If it is still different, call the bank. They may have made a mistake.

When you are done, most of the items in your register will probably be checked off. Now you have to look at the items that are not checked off.

Turn your statement over to the back, and you will find simple directions for balancing your checkbook:

- Start at the top with the ending balance shown on your statement (not the last balance you have in your checkbook register). To that number, you add any deposits listed in your register that are not checked off yet. You add all that up and get another number (A).

- The next step is to look at all your outstanding checks. These are checks you have written that have not been subtracted from your account yet. They will not have a checkmark by them in your register. List all those checks, plus any withdrawals or debit transactions not checked off in your register as well. Add them all together to get one number (B).

- Next, you subtract B from A. This gives you your final balance. If you look at that number, and then flip to the ending balance in your checkbook register, the two numbers should match. That is a balanced checkbook. It means you and the bank agree on all the transactions and on how much is left in your account.

If they don't match, double-check all of your math. If they still don't match and you cannot figure out where you went wrong, call your bank and ask if you can come in for some help. Don't feel stupid. Lots of people have trouble balancing their checkbooks. Bank employees would much rather help you at this point than have you come in six months later with a checkbook you've never gotten to balance a single time.

Start a file for household information. Balance your checkbook every single month and keep the statements in your household file for one year.

Credit Cards

Think long and hard before getting a credit card. They have pros and cons, but they are so frequently abused that often they don't seem worth the risk. The pros are that they help you establish credit, assuming you pay your bill on time each month, and that they give you an emergency option if you have a sudden crisis, such as a huge car repair bill or the need to fly somewhere for a sick family member.

Teens and Credit Cards

About 70% of college kids carry credit cards in their own names, with average monthly balances ranging from more than $500 to almost $2,000. In addition, the number of young people filing for bankruptcy increased by 50% during the 1990s as credit card use among teens became more popular.

(All figures are from *Consumer Finance: College Students and Credit Cards*, U.S. General Accounting Office.)

The cons are that they quickly get you used to the buy now, pay later mentality, and that a new crisis always seems to come up, usually before you have finished paying off the last one. A credit card can also destroy your credit if you don't manage it well, and then you will find it hard to do the things you might really want to do, like finance a car or buy a house. They also cost you money, because credit cards charge you interest on all your purchases. Basically, the credit card company loans you the money to pay for something, and you have to pay back that loan plus interest, often at extremely high rates of 18% to 20%. Other ways of building up your credit exist.

If you do decide to get a credit card, here are tips to staying sane:

- Pay it off in full every month.
- Keep in mind that it is not free money, not matter how easy it feels. You not only have to pay for the item you are buying, you have to pay interest, too.
- If you mean to use your credit card only in emergency, don't even carry it with you. Leave it at home to avoid impulse buying.
- Never let your debt load (all your payments for things you already have—credit cards, car payment, etc.) add up to more than 15% of your income. So, if you make $1,100 per month, your car payment and credit card payments together should not add up to more than $165 per month ($1,100.00 X 0.15 = $165.00).
- Think hard before you buy over the Internet. It is fast and convenient, but the amount you are spending can sneak up on you.

Saving Money

So, you have got that empty savings account just sitting there, right? Now's a good time to start saving money. You might think it's the worst time, because you have so little of it, but it's not. If you try to put extra money into savings, that account will stay exactly the same: empty. The trick is to pay your savings account, which is the same as paying yourself, first.

Many financial advisors suggest trying to save 10% of your income. This may or may not be possible for you, depending on your income and your expenses. Even if you cannot save 10%, even $10 can make a difference. Save $10 per week in a savings account earning 5% interest, and you will have almost $1,700 in three years. That's $1,560 you put in and more than $100 in interest.

Plenty of ways to earn even more interest in various money markets and individual retirement accounts exist, but we are sticking with the basics here. If you have a little more money to save or to invest, talk to a free financial consultant, like the ones at United Way's Consumer Credit offices (see resource listing at the end of this chapter).

You may also find it helpful to have more than one savings account. I often had five different savings accounts going throughout college. The first one was to save up for a new car, the second one was for Christmas, and so on, and the last one was always my emergency fund. If I got really ill and had to miss a week of work, this account hopefully had the money to cover the bills that were due. I could often only contribute a few bucks to each account each week. But somehow I got the stuff I really needed, paid my bills, and kept plugging along. The stuff I never did get (I remember one aqua-colored couch I really wanted), I eventually lost interest in, and I used the money for something else.

Resources

Books

Bamford, J. (2000). *Street wise: A guide for teen investors.* Princeton, NJ: Bloomberg Press.

Bowman-Kruhm, M. (2000). *Money: Save it, manage it, spend it (Teen issues).* Berkeley Heights, NJ: Enslow.

Burkett, L. (1998). *Money management for college students.* Chicago: Moody Press.

Dacyczyn, A. (1999). *The complete tightwad gazette: Promoting thrift as a viable alternative lifestyle.* New York: Random House.

Horowitz, S. (1995). *The penny-pinching hedonist: How to live like royalty with a peasant's pocketbook.* Northampton, MA: Accurate Writing & More.

Taylor-Hough, D. (2000). *A simple choice: A practical guide to saving your time, money and sanity.* Fredonia, WI: Champion Press.

Taylor-Hough, D. (2003). *Frugal living for dummies.* Hoboken, NJ: John Wiley & Sons.

Websites

About.com Financial Planning

http://financialplan.about.com/library/blcollbudget.htm

A budget worksheet for college students.

Bankrate.com

http://www.bankrate.com/brm/news/special/20010425b.asp

Bankrate.com has a printable monthly budget sheet for college kids, too.

Business Owner's Toolkit

http://www.toolkit.cch.com/tools/fambud_m.asp

Although this website is called Business Owner's Toolkit, it has a family monthly budget template you can download to use with Microsoft Excel.

Credit Card Nation

http://www.creditcardnation.com/calculator.html

Loan and credit card payment calculator.

Frugal Fun.com

http://www.frugalfun.com/

Read the archives for ideas for cheap fun and subscribe to a free monthly e-newsletter.

Genus Budget Calculator

http://www.genus.org

Go to this website and click "Personal Finance Calculators" on the far left.

Harvard Medical School

http://www.hms.harvard.edu/finaid/html/detailed_monthly_budget_worksh.html

Harvard Medical School's printable monthly budget sheet.

iVillage.com

http://www.ivillage.co.uk/money/cashflow/

iVillage's British budget online worksheet. Ignore the sign for British currency (£). The numbers will be the same if you use all dollars.

Simple Times

http://hometown.aol.com/dsimple/times.html

Check out this webpage and subscribe to Simple Times newsletter, a twice a month e-newsletter devoted to simplicity and frugality.

United Way's Consumer Credit Counseling Service

http://www.cccsatl.org/

United Way's Consumer Credit program offers free budget and housing counseling, money management, credit and consumer education programs, debt management, and a repayment program. Telephone counseling is also available to anyone who calls 1-800-251-2227.

Women's Finance.com

http://www.womens-finance.com/studentbudget.shtml

This site has a good monthly budget sheet for college students (men or women).

CHAPTER 9

In Training
Taking Care of Your Body

I know it is hard to think about the long-term effects of not taking care of yourself when you are a teenager. Cancer, wrinkles, obesity, osteoporosis—all these possibilities are likely decades in the future. You are probably so busy that you have trouble keeping track of things happening next week, let alone 20 years from now.

This doesn't mean you shouldn't take care of yourself, however. Aside from the fact that you will be in much better shape in your 30s and beyond, you have plenty of more immediate reasons to take care of your mind and body. If you treat your body well, you will have more energy, be in a better mood, and feel more fit. You won't have days of hangovers and nausea, and you won't get too big for your clothes. You will get sick less often and miss fewer paychecks and fun times. You will also feel less stressed and will be better able to handle your hectic life.

Basically, if you take good care of your body, it will take good care of you. It won't collapse on you when you occasionally eat too much. It will be up to the challenge, whether that means running across campus for class, Rollerblading to work, or going whitewater rafting. It'll obediently fall asleep every night, but it will also allow you to function on those days when you are up too late studying or working and don't get enough sleep.

What Your Body Needs

So how do you take good care of yourself? You need to give your body three basic things: sleep, good food, and activity.

Getting enough sleep is crucial to functioning well and feeling good. If you work until 1 A.M. every morning, scheduling 8 A.M. classes is a mistake. By the time you get home from work and unwind, it will be 2 A.M. You will probably need to get up by at least 7 A.M. to make your 8 A.M. class. Five hours of sleep a night is cutting it pretty short.

Your best bet is to arrange your schedule so that you can get about seven hours of sleep per night. Of course, you are in charge of your life now. Just because you plan on going to bed at midnight and getting up at 7 A.M. every day doesn't mean it is written in stone. You might be up late studying for finals for an entire week, not getting to sleep until 2 A.M. If you are not already sleep-deprived, your body might be able to handle that, or you might feel like going to bed early all the next week to get caught back up.

The bottom line is that you know how much sleep you need to feel good. Look at your schedule and make sure that you can get it.

I know you've already heard about healthy food. You have probably been told about the food pyramid, the food groups, nutritional labeling, fat grams, and a whole lot more. If you already try to eat healthy, great! If you are a typical junk-food-loving teen, like I was, here are a few very simple tips to eat healthier:

- Drink a lot of water (6–8 glasses per day) and not so much soda.
- Eat some fruits and veggies—apples and bananas make good portable snacks.
- Try to avoid junk food when possible. Does this mean you shouldn't ever have it? No, of course not. But if you eat leftover pizza for breakfast, burger and fries for lunch, and cheesesticks and buffalo wings for dinner, well, your body is going to let you know that you are not taking care of it eventually, by getting lots bigger or feeling ill.
- Keep water and healthy snacks with you. I like to freeze a big 32 oz. water bottle so that as it thaws throughout the day, I always have ice cold water. It is smart to carry around some crackers and other durable, halfway healthy snacks so that the vending machines aren't calling your name by 10 a.m.
- Get milk. Drink milk each day or get calcium through yogurt or low-fat cheese. Dark green leafy veggies, like spinach, broccoli, and kale, are also good sources of calcium. Canned fish and cooked dried beans and peas can help you meet your body's needs as well. Lots of foods now come in calcium-enriched versions. You can buy orange juice, cereals, and apple juice all with added calcium. Aim for three servings a day of calcium-rich foods.

Activity is the third thing your body really needs. If you are working and going to school, and you drive a car everywhere you go, it can be tough to work in activity during your day. The latest guidelines from the National Academies' Food and Nutrition Board recommend an hour of activity daily to stay healthy (*Project: Dietary Reference Intakes for Macronutrients,* see http://www.iom.edu/report.asp?id=4340). Plenty of other national organizations agree that research supports that recommendation. Wow—I can't find the time for that much! But anything you can do is better than nothing.

If you don't have the time or inclination to build activity into your schedule by way of a gym, a sport, or a scheduled workout, look for ways to sneak it in:

- Buy a pedometer. For about $15, you can buy a pedometer to clip to your belt. Aim for 10,000 steps per day.
- Get out with friends. When you are looking for something to do with your friends, choose something active. Go dancing. Go for a walk. Go swimming.
- Each night, look at your schedule for the next day. Is there something you can do to add some activity to it? Maybe you can walk to the drugstore a mile away to pick up your pictures instead of driving there like you usually do. When you meet your friends for lunch between classes, you can walk afterward while you chat. Do 15 minutes' worth of sit-ups and bicep curls before you shower in the morning.

The point is that even if you cannot do an entire hour's worth, every little bit you can do will make your body healthier.

Expert Advice:
Fitting Activity into Your Day

Having trouble fitting exercise into your day? Here are a few suggestions from Margaret J. Blythe, MD, Director of Adolescent Clinical Services at Indiana University:

- Take the stairs when possible (no matter how many floors) both up and down.

- No remote! Change the television channel by walking to it.

- Better still, limit television to one program a day, and take that walk.

- Walk fast, don't amble.

- Take a longer route to class or work.

What Your Body Does Not Need

We've talked about what your body needs. Here are three things it doesn't need: alcohol, drugs, and tobacco. No surprises here, right?

Alcohol and drugs can hurt your life in so many ways. Using them can lower your grades, make you lose your job, send you to jail, break up your relationships, and literally end your life.

Will one beer do all that? Of course not. Although it could do some of it, like make you lose your job and send you to jail, if you were found drinking on the job and were underage, for example.

But choosing a lifestyle that involves a lot of drinking and any amount of doing drugs is not going to get you where you want to be. This does not put you in control of your life, instead, it hands the control over to the drugs and alcohol.

We've talked about what hard work living independently is. It is impossible to be independent in a drunken stupor. Any time you are not clear-headed, you are relying on other people to take care of you. You are relying on them to not let you drive, to not let you jump off an eight-story building, to not let you throw up all over your new car. If you really want to be in charge of your own life, you have to accept that responsibility. Getting drunk and doing drugs will just prove to people that you are not mature enough to handle your own life.

Tobacco is also a danger to your way of life. Although it's illegal to buy cigarettes before you are 18 (21 in a few states), smoking itself is not illegal. In fact, more than 3 million teens in the United States smoke. Just today, more than 4,000 kids tried their

Will It or Won't It?

Remember the simple technique for working toward goals? Just ask yourself, Will doing this help me reach my goal or won't it? You can use that same technique to improve your health. At the fast-food joint, ask yourself, Will ordering that five-pound cheeseburger help me stay healthy, or is there something a bit better I can get? You might find yourself ordering the turkey sandwich. Or, when you are about to go for that second alcoholic drink, ask yourself that question again. This simple question can at least make you more aware of your choices. It doesn't really put any restrictions on you, and if you have eaten healthy all week, you might just feel you deserve that five-pound cheeseburger! But by asking yourself to consider your choices, you make it easier to start changing your eating habits. Remember, you are not aiming for perfection. Just try to make healthier choices than you would have a month ago.

first cigarette. About one-third of them will die prematurely from a smoking-caused illness. Don't be part of that group.

Almost 15% of high school boys use chewing tobacco. If the thought of lung cancer, emphysema, and throat cancer doesn't scare you (and it will, if you look at some pictures and case studies), think of the more practical, immediate reasons to stay away from tobacco:

- It's expensive. Do you have money to burn, literally, on cigarettes? Sit down and figure out how much you spend every week on cigarettes or chew. Multiply that by 52. That's how much you spend per year on smoking or chewing. Can't you think of other things you need to spend that money on?

- It makes you smell bad. Even if smokers haven't had a puff in two days, their breath, their hair, their clothes, and everything about them seems permanently perfumed with cigarette smoke. Their cars and apartments always smell bad, too. I realize that it doesn't smell bad to people who actually smoke, but trying to form a friendship or a romance with someone who doesn't smoke might be tough.

- It is also bad for your teeth. Chewing-tobacco users are four times more likely than nonusers to get cavities and gingivitis, which can lead to tooth and bone loss. Smokers are also more prone to gingivitis than nonsmokers. Nicotine from cigarettes and chew also leaves a yellowish-brown stain on your teeth.

You have lots of good reasons not to smoke. If you want to quit and don't know how, ask your doctor. Also, call the university nearest you and see if they know of any stop-smoking studies (smoking-cessation studies) that you can participate in.

By keeping drugs, alcohol, and tobacco out of your body, you are remaining in control of your life and helping ensure that your body will be healthy now and for a long time to come.

When You Are Sick

Everyone gets sick now and then. The difference is that as an independent person, you have more responsibilities. You can't count on your brother to bring home your missed schoolwork, or your mom to call in sick to work for you. Nobody is going to cook you your favorite dinner or take care of your chores just because you're sick. That's one thing that stinks about being independent!

When you get sick, you have to balance taking care of yourself with meeting your various commitments: work and school, mainly.

First, take care of yourself. With most illnesses, this means getting extra rest and extra fluids. Obviously, follow any directions your doctor gives you, too. If you start feeling run down, don't wait until you are horribly sick. Cancel a couple of nights' worth of social plans, get some extra sleep, and make a real effort to eat and drink healthy stuff. Taking some extra vitamin C would be good, too.

Also, go to the doctor when your symptoms call for it. Being tough and trying to ride it out might just lead to a longer illness. If it is something besides a cold, a trip to the doctor might mean you get treatment faster and feel better faster.

Second, address your obligations. Keep in mind that bosses and teachers like to have plenty of notice about things, and it is nice to ask them instead of tell them. Look at what you have going on the next few days and think about what can be put off and what cannot. Is your brother getting married Saturday? He is not going to change that because you have a sinus infection. Were you planning to get the oil changed in your car tonight? That can wait until you feel better. Make yourself a list of what you absolutely have to get done today, do it, and then crawl into bed. Here's how to make that list.

Check out your work schedule. If you think you are going to miss work because you're sick, call your boss right away. Even if you don't work until tomorrow, if you are feeling horrible today, call and give him or her a heads up that you might be out sick tomorrow. That way, he or she can think about who can fill in for you. This will leave your boss feeling much kinder toward you than if you call him or her 10 minutes before your shift begins and say you are not coming in.

Next look at your school schedule. What has to be done? If you have an exam in two days that cannot be made up, devote any extra energy to studying for it. That means read through your notes for an hour before you crawl into bed.

Make it to school if you can, but if you cannot, call and leave a message at the office or the individual teacher's work number explaining that you are missing class because you're sick. Call someone from each class and see if they will make you a copy of their notes and pick up any handouts for you. It is great to have the name and phone number of at least one person in each of your classes for just this reason. Just be ready to return the favor when someone else is sick.

If you are sick enough that you're going to miss more than one or two days, definitely call the school and let each of your teachers know. As soon as you feel better, touch base with each teacher to see how to handle the make-up work.

Third, take care of your personal and financial obligations. What have you promised people that you will do? Do you have bills that are due in three days? Write the checks and get them in the mail before you lie down. Are you supposed to go out with friends to Christmas shop tonight? Call and beg off, explaining that you are sick. Did you promise to give your neighbor a ride to work today? Call and explain that you're not feeling that great, and find out if anyone else might be able to take him. If not, drag your butt out and give him the ride, unless you're sick enough that you don't feel safe behind the wheel. The idea is to get rid of as many obligations as you can without dumping stuff on people and throwing your commitments out the window.

Once you figure out what you have to get done, see if you can get any help with things. If you need medicine, ask if your pharmacy delivers. Many do, for free (although you should tip the delivery person a couple of bucks). If you have got that big exam but you can't concentrate on the notes, see if a friend will come quiz you. If you are really lucky (and have made good choices in friends), your friend will go through a drive-through and pick you up dinner, too, if you're hungry.

While you are sick, try to keep up with the most important commitments in your life. Otherwise, your work and school and personal relationships will be in a mess by the time you feel better; however, be realistic about what you can do. As much as you can, baby yourself. You will be back up to snuff in a few days, catching up on the things you put off.

Mental Health

You need to take care of your mental health as well as your physical health. Depression among teens is frighteningly common, with girls more likely to develop it than boys. According to the National Mental Health Association (www.nmha.org/children/children_mh_matters/depression.cfm), 3 million teens in our country have depression, or about one out of every eight teens.

The symptoms: If you feel sad, empty, hopeless, guilty, or just blah on a regular basis, that may be depression. I am not talking about a bad day or a bad week here and there. Depression is an underlying feeling that is with you all the time, even during good times. Other common symptoms include headaches and stomachaches, sleep problems (either too much or too little sleep), lack of energy, and thinking about death or suicide.

Depression can be very scary, especially if you have never had any treatment for it and you think that you are just different or weird. Almost 2,000 teenagers kill themselves every year, and by far the number one cause of suicide is untreated depression.

The good news is that depression can be treated. Contact the National Mental Health Association (NMHA) or the American Academy of Child and Adolescent Psychiatry for more information on teen depression and other mental illnesses (see resource list at the end of this chapter). In addition, your school and your doctor probably have resources available for you on this topic.

The most important thing to remember is that depression is not anything to be embarrassed about. I have several family members with depression or related conditions, and we all regularly

> **By the Numbers**
>
> **Mental Illness and Kids**
>
> Here are the estimated numbers from NIMH and NMHA of kids with the following mental illnesses
>
> Clinical depression—About one out of eight adolescents
>
> ADHD—As many as 5% of kids
>
> Bipolar disorder—Up to 1.1 million kids
>
> Anxiety disorders—As many as 10% of all kids

share our experiences with others. As with many other mental illnesses, doctors and scientists now know that depression has a biological cause. In other words, a chemical imbalance is causing you to feel the way you do, and it can be corrected. You do not have to put up with feelings of despair.

Other common illnesses among teens include attention deficit disorder and attention deficit/hyperactivity disorder (ADHD), both of which cause difficulty focusing on tasks. With ADHD, you might also feel restless and unable to stop yourself from fidgeting.

According to the National Institute of Mental Health (NIMH), more than 80% of kids with mental illness do not receive treatment (www.nimh.gov/publicat/childqa.cfm). Don't let yourself be part of that group. If you feel like you have more trouble handling daily life or have more fears and worries than other people, or like you are just not as connected to other people as you should be, call a doctor and get checked out.

NMHA has an online, free, private depression-screening questionnaire at http://www.depression-screening.org/. NMHA's website also contains lots of helpful links for more information, finding treatment, and other mental health topics.

Your Medical History

Start a file for your medical information. As you move around, change schools, and change doctors over the years, it will become hard to remember who tested you for allergies, what that medication was that made you throw up, and when you broke your arm.

Begin with Worksheets 6 and 7. If you are on good terms with your parents, ask them for the information on your medical history. Otherwise, if you know who your pediatrician was, request the information directly from that office. Fill in as much as you can. Keep your medical and dental history updated by copying Worksheet 7 and filling it in as you go along. You do not need to enter every cold or headache you get, just the more major ill-

Worksheet 6

My Medical History

Name: _____

Date of birth: ____/____/____ Place of birth: _____ Weight at birth: _____

Height at birth: _____ Normal pregnancy and delivery? _____

Childhood vaccinations *(These are given in series, and you should have several dates for most of these):*

    Oral polio: _____

    MMR (Measles, Mumps, Rubella): _____

    Chicken pox (varicella): _____

    HIB: _____

    DTP (Diptheria, Tetanus, Pertussis): _____

    Hepatitis B: _____

    Other: _____

Childhood illnesses, injuries, and surgeries

    Illness: _____ Date: ____/____/____ Treated By: _____

    Illness: _____ Date: ____/____/____ Treated By: _____

    Illness: _____ Date: ____/____/____ Treated By: _____

    Illness: _____ Date: ____/____/____ Treated By: _____

    Illness: _____ Date: ____/____/____ Treated By: _____

    Illness: _____ Date: ____/____/____ Treated By: _____

Has anyone in your family had the following? List who, at what age, and how serious it was.

    Cancer: _____

    Diabetes: _____

    Heart problems: _____

    Stroke: _____

    Allergies: _____

    Asthma: _____

    Thyroid disorder: _____

    High blood pressure: _____

    Depression: _____

    Mental illness: _____

    Kidney disease: _____

    Substance abuse: _____

    Tuberculosis: _____

    Headaches: _____

Maternal grandmother still living? Y N   Died at what age? _____ Cause? _____

Maternal grandfather still living? Y N   Died at what age? _____ Cause? _____

Mother still living? Y N   Died at what age? _____ Cause? _____

Paternal grandmother still living? Y N   Died at what age? _____ Cause? _____

Paternal grandfather still living? Y N   Died at what age? _____ Cause? _____

Father still living? Y N   Died at what age? _____ Cause? _____

Worksheet 7

Medical and Dental Notes

DATE	ILLNESS/INJURY	DOCTOR/HOSPITAL	TREATMENT	NOTES

Expert Advice: Do You Need to See a Doctor?

It gets frustrating spending cash on doctor's appointments, only to hear, "Get some rest and drink lots of fluids." You might even be tempted to avoid doctor's offices entirely; however, the following symptoms can all be signs of problems requiring medical treatment. If you have one of them, it's time to call the doctor:

- Abdominal pain
- Unusually severe headaches that may have symptoms such as nausea or vomiting
- Burning with urination
- Missed period
- Chest pain
- Shortness of breath
- Fainting
- Vaginal discharge with itch, odor, or pain
- Fever lasting longer than 72 hours
- Vomiting repeatedly for longer than 24 hours

—*Margaret J. Blythe, MD,*
Director of Adolescent Clinical Services, Indiana University

nesses and injuries. Be sure to get the address and the phone number of the office you were treated at so that you can get more complete records in the future if you need them.

Pregnancy: How to Avoid It

If you do not want to become pregnant, you have two options. Don't have sex, or use birth control. Birth control methods include birth control pills, birth control shots, condoms, diaphragms, birth control implants, spermicides, and female condoms.

Some of these methods (birth control pills, implants, and diaphragms) require visits to the doctor or prescriptions. Others (condoms, spermicides, and female condoms) require only an over-the-counter purchase.

Condoms offer the additional benefit of protection against HIV/AIDS and other sexually transmitted diseases.

For a good list of the birth control methods available to teens, check out http://www.plannedparenthood.org/ or call their national hotline, 1-800-230-PLAN.

Sexually Transmitted Infections (STIs)

Most teens, like most adults, don't know a whole lot about STIs other than AIDS...until they get one. Basically, an STI is an infection spread from one person to another through sexual activity.

Here's the rundown of some common STIs:

- **AIDS/HIV.** HIV disease is a viral infection that eventually leads to AIDS. It breaks down the body's immune system and makes a person more susceptible to other diseases. People can spread HIV through blood, semen, breast milk, and vaginal secretions. Sexual activity and needle-sharing for drug use are the most common ways that HIV is spread. We have no cure for AIDS, although researchers are developing better treatments. You cannot tell if someone else has HIV. Most people who are HIV-positive don't even know it. Many people have no symptoms at all until it develops into AIDS, usually many years later. The test for HIV is a blood test, and it is a good idea for sexually active teens to get tested at least once a year.

A Well-Stocked Medicine Cabinet

The following are some basic supplies to have on hand:

- adhesive bandages

- gauze

- adhesive tape

- pain reliever (ibuprofen or acetaminophen)

- decongestant for stuffy noses

- cough syrup

- antihistamine for itchy eyes and runny noses

- syrup of ipecac (for inducing vomiting *only* if your poison control office tells you to)

- elastic stretch bandages for sprains and twists

- a chemical cold pack and heat pack

- alcohol swabs

- hydrogen peroxide

- an eye dropper,

- an oral syringe, and

- a good first-aid or health manual like *Family Health and Emergency Guide* (Time-Life Books, 1999). This will tell you how to stock your medicine cabinet, how to tell what might be wrong with you, how to treat it, and when you should see the doctor.

- **Gonorrhea.** This is a common bacterial infection spread through sexual contact (vaginal, anal, or oral sex). Neither intercourse nor ejaculation is required to spread this infection. The infection can then spread to other parts of your body, such as your eyes. Symptoms for men include burning urination and penile discharge, which usually appear a few days after infection but can take up to 30 days to show up. Many women show no symptoms. Gonorrhea can be cured by antibiotics, and untreated gonorrhea can lead to more serious health problems, like pelvic inflammatory disease for women and infertility for men. It can even spread to the blood and joints and be life threatening. Latex condoms can help protect you from gonorrhea.
- **Genital herpes.** This is a viral disease that causes painful blisters around the genitals or anus. Once a person has herpes, he or she will have outbreaks about four to five times a year, although they usually become shorter and less severe. Herpes is transmitted during sexual activity, sometimes even when the infected person does not appear to be having a herpes outbreak. We have no cure for herpes at this time, but antiviral medications can help shorten the outbreaks. Condoms provide some protection against infection.
- **Genital warts.** These warts are caused by the human papilloma virus. These soft, flesh-colored warts can be spread by vaginal, anal, and oral sex. They are painless but itchy. Consistent use of condoms is decent protection for the sexually active teen. Genital warts can be treated with chemicals applied directly to the warts, with cryotherapy (freezing them off), or with surgery. For some people, especially smokers, the warts recur several months after treatment. If they are not treated, they might continue to grow and spread.
- **Syphilis.** Syphilis is a bacterial disease. It is spread through contact with a syphilis sore, which generally occurs on the genitals, anus, and mouth. Syphilis first appears 10 to 90 days after infection as a small, round, painless sore, or more than one. The sore usually lasts three to six weeks and then goes away, however, if it is not treated, the infection progresses to the second stage, which usually involves faint rashes and possibly a sore throat, swollen glands, achiness, headaches, and weight loss. During the first and second stages, syphilis is highly contagious. If it is still not treated, it moves on to late-stage syphilis. At this point, the disease is not obvious, but it is still spreading inside your body. Long-term effects can include damage to the heart, liver, bones, and brain, and eventually can cause paralysis, blindness, and death. Early treatment with penicillin is crucial, because treatment cannot repair damage already done. Condoms provide some, but not complete, protection. You cannot always tell if someone has syphilis, because sores can be hidden inside the vagina, rectum, or mouth.
- **Chlamydia.** This is a bacterial infection that affects women's reproductive organs. It is transmitted during vaginal, anal, or oral sex. It is called a silent disease because it has few symptoms, and untreated infections can result in irreversible damage, including infertility. Chlamydia can be easily treated with antibiotics. To help prevent the spread of Chlamydia, use a condom every time you have sex, and don't have multiple sex partners. You should also get a screening test once a year.
- **Pubic lice** (Pediculosis pubis). Sometimes called crabs, pubic lice are highly contagious. Unlike most other STIs, they can be spread by contact with infected clothing, furniture, bedding, and toilet seats, in addition to any kind of sex-

ual contact. They look pale gray, but when swollen with blood, they appear darker. They are itchy and constantly bite you, leaving small bluish spots. Genital itching is the most common symptom of this STI. You can buy over-the-counter medicine called pediculicide for pubic lice, so you do not have to go to a doctor for this one, unless you are not sure what infection you've got. The shampoo usually works, but if not, see your doctor for different and stronger medicine.

- **Trichomoniasis.** This is caused by a common single-celled parasite. It is spread through genital-to-genital contact. Women can catch it from men or women, whereas men seem to only be able to catch it from women. This is the most common STI in young, sexually active women. For women, symptoms are a smelly, yellowish-green vaginal discharge; possibly painful intercourse or urination; and itching. Most men do not show symptoms, although they might have penile discharge or irritation and burning urination or ejaculation.

An estimated 10% of American citizens will have an STI at some time in their life. More than 3 million teens get a new STI every year.

Protecting Yourself from STIs

The only 100% surefire protection from an STI is to not be sexually active or to engage in intimate sex play with other people. If you choose to be sexually active, please take the following steps to keep yourself healthy. Many STIs can have long-term effects on your body:

- Use a condom every time you have sex.

- Ask your partner if he or she has any STIs. Be aware, however, that many people lie about this.

- Examine yourself regularly. Use a mirror and check for any new sores, spots, and so on.

- Go to a doctor for an examination at least once a year, and request that you be checked for any STIs.

- Limit the number of partners you have. A person in a monogamous relationship (in which you are faithful and have only one partner) is less vulnerable to STIs.

STI Symptoms to Watch for

Different STIs cause varying symptoms. If you are sexually active, even if you do not actually have intercourse, you should see a doctor if you have any of the following symptoms:

- abnormal or smelly discharge from the vagina, penis, or rectum
- bleeding
- blisters
- a burning sensation while urinating
- growths
- itching
- irritation
- odor
- pain
- painful intercourse
- pus
- rash
- sores
- swelling
- tenderness
- a change in urine
- a vaginal yeast infection
- warts

—*Adapted from Planned Parenthood information* (From phone interview with Jon Knowles of Planned Parenthood on November 21, 2002.)

Trichomoniasis can cause an increased chance of contracting HIV on exposure, and it can cause delivery dangers in pregnant women. Drug treatment can cure the problem in women, but the woman and her partner should both be tested so she does not get reinfected.

Try not to be embarrassed about going to the doctor. Be honest about your sexual activity: how often you have had sex, how many partners you've had, and so on. Your doctor has likely treated hundreds of teens with whatever you have. It is important that you take good care of yourself, so bite the bullet and make the appointment.

Health Insurance

Health insurance is a program in which a person or his or her employer pays for a policy, and that policy gives the covered person (that's you) access to less expensive health care.

Health insurance companies work in two basic ways. If they are health maintenance organizations, or HMOs, they tend to have their own medical centers and doctors, and you go to one of those centers when you are sick or injured. Health Partners, Blue Care, and Group Health are a few examples of HMOs. When you go to that medical center, you might not have to pay anything for your appointment, or you might have to pay a copay. It just depends on the coverage for your policy.

Other insurance policies let you pick your own doctors, but these policies involve more paperwork. Sometimes you can see any certified doctor you want, and as long as the treatment is one that the insurance company covers, they will pay a certain percentage of the treatment, usually about 80%. That means if you see a doctor, and the appointment costs $100, it is going to cost you $20. If the appointment is only $50, you only have to pay $10. If you run up a $1,000 treatment bill (which is not hard to do once lab work and x-rays come into the picture), however, you will be responsible for $200.

Definitions: A co-pay is the amount you pay every time you visit the doctor, often $10 to $20.

Sometimes these non-HMO companies have a list of preferred providers. If you see a doctor on their list, they pay a higher percentage, like 80% or 90%. If you choose to see a doctor who is not on their list, they might pay only 60% to 70%.

With all non-HMO companies, you should check to see if the doctor you are seeing will bill your insurance company first. Otherwise, that doctor is going to expect you to pay the entire bill, whether it's $50 or $1,000, and then you will get your money reimbursed (you hope) by your insurance company. That means more money out of your pocket, at least temporarily, and more paperwork and phone calls for you.

So, how do you get health insurance? I know you're sick of hearing this, but this is a really complicated issue. Health insurance is complicated even for adults, let alone for teens, especially if you are not legally eman-

By the Numbers: According to the Center for Adolescent Health and the Law (English, Morreale, & Stinnett, 1999), approximately 4 million American adolescents are uninsured. Not only that, but more than half of those teens are eligible for insurance through Medicaid or the State Children's Health Insurance Program (www.adolescenthealthlaw.org).

cipated. If you are not emancipated, you kind of fall into that gray area where the government assumes your family is responsible for you, but you know that's not true.

To find out if you are eligible for any government-paid insurance, call your local department of social services or state department of health. Each state has its own rules. Your guidance counselor or another adult on your coaching team also might be able to help you look into this. Insurance is ridiculously confusing, and this is one area in which adult help will make things much simpler for you. Talk with the adult helping you to try to understand your options. Health insurance is something you will need to deal with the rest of your life, so you might as well start learning about it now.

If you call 1-877-543-7669 (1-877-KIDS-NOW), your call will be put through to a department in your state that handles low-cost or free health insurance for kids. You can also visit the website at http://www.insurekidsnow.gov/. From that site, you can link to your state's program. This is an excellent program to check out. This program is run by the federal government, but each state chooses which department will implement the program.

Also, you might be eligible for insurance through your job. Many jobs only offer insurance coverage to full-time employees, but some offer coverage to those who work 30 or even only 20 hours per week. Another option for health insurance is through your school. High schools and colleges offer health insurance plans to students at reduced rates.

Employers and schools can offer reduced rates because they buy so many policies that insurance companies charge them less. If you try to buy insurance coverage on your own from a private insurance company, you will pay hundreds of dollars per month, which you probably cannot afford.

Usually, you will pay a monthly premium for your policy. This premium is the monthly cost to you. Very few employers pay the entire cost so that the insurance is completely free to you. Although the expense may hurt your budget, having insurance is really crucial these days. With prescription prices skyrocketing and doctor's fees no small matter, your insurance will pay for itself, even if you only see a doctor occasionally. Should you have a serious illness or injury, you will more than make up the cost of your monthly premiums in a short time.

Resources

Books

Goldstein, M. A., & Goldstein, M. M. (2000). *Boys into men: Staying healthy through the teen years.* Westport, CT: Greenwood.

Lopez, R. I. (20020. *The teen health book: A parent's guide to adolescent health and well-being.* New York: W.W. Norton.

Hotlines

Centers for Disease Control and Prevention

National AIDS Hotline

1-800-342-AIDS (1-800-342-2437)

Spanish: 1-800-344-7432

TTY: 1-800-243-7889

National Sexually Transmitted Disease Hotline

1-800-227-8922

Planned Parenthood

> 1-800-230-PLAN (7526)
>
> This number will connect you with your local Planned Parenthood office, which can set up an appointment for you or point you toward other community resources for all your questions about sexual health and STIs.

Websites

American Academy of Child and Adolescent Psychiatry

> http://www.aacap.org/
>
> Lots of mental health information in the "Facts for Families" section.

Healthfinder

> http://www.healthfinder.gov/
>
> This website is run by the U.S. government and offers health information, insurance information, medical providers in your area, and so on.

Insure Kids Now

> http://www.insurekidsnow.gov/
>
> This is a free or low-cost health insurance program for kids 18 and younger who are not already insured through other programs. You can also call 1-877-543-7669 (1-877-KIDS-NOW).

Medem

> http://www.medem.com
>
> Type the medical topic you want to learn more about in the Search Medem box, and find fact sheets and studies from the American Academy of Pediatrics and other reputable organizations.

National Mental Health Association

> http://www.nmha.org/
>
> You can try this website or call 1-800-969-NMHA (1-800-969-6642).

Planned Parenthood

> http://www.plannedparenthood.org/index.html
>
> This website offers fact sheets and lots of information about all areas of sexual health.

Start Healthy, Stay Healthy

> http://www.cbpp.org/shsh/index.html
>
> *The Start Healthy, Stay Healthy* campaign to find health care for kids can hook you up with health resources in your state. They have links to online applications and information for many states, and if your state is not listed, you can request an application by mail or call 202/408-1080.

Teenwire

> http://www.teenwire.com/index.asp
>
> This is Planned Parenthood's website just for teens.

United Way's First Call for Help

> http://national.unitedway.org/
>
> The phone number of 211 is available in some parts of the country as the direct line to United Way's First Call for Help. This can be a great resource if you do not know who to call about issues like housing, insurance, safety, mental and physical health, and so on. The counselors on the phone will refer you to the local resources that can help you. If 211 does not work in your area, log on to the website to find your local number, or call information, 411, and ask for the local United Way number.

CHAPTER 10

Safety Gear
Protecting Yourself in a
Dangerous World

When you were born, lots of people looked out for your safety. They gave you shots to help you avoid diseases, put plugs in the outlets so you wouldn't electrocute yourself, and put up baby gates to keep you from falling down the stairs. As you got older, safety precautions took another form. Teachers talked about good touching and bad touching, and parents gave you curfews so that you would get home safely. Your house may have had a security alarm to keep everyone inside safe from unwelcome visitors.

Now that you are going to be taking care of yourself, you need to think about how to keep yourself safe. Like most teenagers, you might feel invincible. Danger and death might seem like things that only old people worry about. But they're not.

Take a good look at your life and see where you feel most vulnerable. Maybe part of the reason you are moving out is that you don't feel safe at home. Good for you! But make sure you don't put yourself into an equally dangerous position somewhere else. Here are some situations in which teens often face dangers: while driving, on the job, on dates, at home, at school, and in urban areas. These are not all of the possible dangerous places in your life, but these are the most common. The dangers range from rape to theft, sexual harassment, mugging, fire, and lawsuits.

Enough of scaring you with the bad news. Let's talk about the good news, which is that you can do a lot to keep yourself safe.

Job Safety

You may have worried that your job will be boring or not pay enough, but you might not have thought about it being dangerous. Every year, about 70 teens die from workplace injuries, and about 70,000 more have injuries serious enough to require emergency room treatment. Motor vehicles are the biggest on-the-job danger. A job that requires driving, such as pizza delivery or newspaper delivery, greatly increases your time on the road and increases your chances of being in a car accident. Working in an area where cars and other vehicles are common, such as road maintenance or a gas station, is also dangerous.

By the Numbers

For every mile driven, a 16- to 19-year-old is four times more likely than an older driver to be involved in a crash, so it makes sense that jobs involving driving are the most dangerous for teens.

Other serious job dangers include heavy machinery accidents (working on a farm or with construction equipment), electrocution (house painting, tree trimming, pool cleaning), homicide (convenience store/gas station night work, motel housekeeping, door-to-door sales), falls (painting, construction, roofing, tree trimming), burns (restaurants), and hazardous lifting (warehouse work, furniture delivery, baling hay).

Be aware that you have the right to work in a safe environment. Many teens are injured because they do not know the proper way to run a certain machine or complete a certain procedure. You have the right to be trained to do your job safely.

All of this may seem so boring, so typically adult—worrying about something that might never happen. Teens who have died or been permanently disabled, however, make the danger impossible to dismiss. Talk to your employers about job safety. Make sure you know emergency procedures. Do you know how to cut off the electricity in an electrical emergency? Is there an alarm button to summon police? Do you know how to safely use every piece of equipment?

Another common job danger is sexual harassment. This may not result in bodily injury, but it is against the law and you don't have to put up with it. Sexual harassment, basically, is any behavior by another person (whether they are of the opposite sex or not) that is sexual in nature and that affects your job. Someone might say that you can only keep your job if you sleep with him or her, or someone might tell you, "You look hot in that outfit." If it makes you feel uncomfortable, then it's sexual harassment. Sexual harassment can be verbal comments or physical actions, like touching you when you don't want to be touched. It can even be things like telling dirty jokes.

If someone says or does something that makes you uncomfortable, your first step is to tell that person directly, "Don't do that. I don't like it." This can be tough to do, especially if you are someone who doesn't like confrontations, but do it anyway. You deserve your own protection. Then you should file a grievance with your employer. Your employer should support you and step in to discuss things with the person who harassed you. If your harasser is your supervisor, go to the owner of the company. If it is the owner or you do not know how to contact the owner, contact the Equal Employment Opportunity Office to file a grievance.

Obviously, sexual harassment is a subjective thing. What one person feels is flirting another person can feel is threatening. Trust your gut. If being around a certain person at work makes you uncomfortable because of comments or physical actions, you are being harassed. On the other hand, if a person asks you out on a date once and then leaves you alone when you turn him or her down, that is probably not sexual harassment.

Home Security

Home is a place where you should always feel safe. Here are some good habits to get into to keep yourself and your belongings protected:

Home Safety Checklist

Use this checklist to see how safe your home is. Follow the directions for inexpensive ways to make your apartment more secure:

Doors:

- Do you have a peephole?
- Is the door solid wood or metal?
- Do you have a dead-bolt (the kind of lock with a steel bar that slides across when it's locked)?
- If your front and back doors don't pass the test, install peepholes and ask the property manager if they will put on a heavy-duty door. They probably won't, but it's worth a try. Do insist that they change to a dead-bolt lock, even if you have to pay for the lock. It will cost you about $50.
- Install (or ask a handy buddy to install) motion-sensor lights at both your doors. These are relatively inexpensive, generally $15 to $30 for a basic light, and are easy to install if you already have a regular light there. They will light up brightly whenever someone walks up to your doors.
- Put a sawed-down broomstick or heavy dowel in the track of the sliding glass door to keep the door from being pushed open.

Windows:

- Do you have sturdy windows with locks that allow you to open them but lock them so that they cannot be opened all the way?
- If you don't have good window locks, or if you need your windows open to catch the breeze, you can create pin locks. Just drill a hole at a 45-degree angle through both the inner and outer frame. Then, insert a double-headed nail or duplex nail into it. Drill a second hole with the window open about eight inches. That way, you can pin the window open so that it cannot be opened any farther.

- Lock the doors, even when you are home.
- Make sure the windows have locks.
- Have discussions with your roommate. If you don't trust his or her friends, it is time for a good heart-to-heart.
- Don't advertise what you have. If you go around bragging about your huge CD collection, that makes you more vulnerable to a break-in.
- Call the police! If you feel unsafe or think someone might be in your apartment, don't go in! Call the police. When I was in college, my roommate and I heard noises above us, as if someone was in the attic. We called the cops and stood there, feeling stupid, while a petite woman cop climbed up the ladder to the attic. Nobody was up there, but she and her partner reassured us repeatedly. They would rather get called to check things out than to process a crime scene.
- Don't hide a key under the mat, in the flowerpot, or on the door ledge. Instead, ask a trusted neighbor to keep one, as well as an adult who could come bail you out if you got locked out.

Expert Advice: Burglary Prevention Tips from ADT Security Systems

- If you have double-hung windows, bolt the upper and lower sashes together or insert a metal bar in the track to prevent opening.

- To secure sliding glass doors, add a bolt lock or use a charley bar to block the door closed.

- Most home burglaries occur between 8:00 A.M. and 5:00 P.M., so get in the habit of always locking all doors and windows whenever you go out.

- According to the FBI, more burglaries occur in July and August than in any other months.

- Never leave an answering machine message indicating you are not at home. Instead, just say you "can't come to the phone."

- Use timers to turn lights, televisions, and sound systems on and off at different times to give your home a lived-in look when you're away.

- Install motion-detecting outdoor floodlights around your home. Remember to mount them high enough to prevent intruders from disabling them.

- If your community has a Neighborhood Watch Program, join it. If it does not, start one.

- Report any suspicious people or vehicles to your local police.

- Get to know your neighbors.

- Do not let mail, newspapers, or flyers accumulate while you are away, tipping off criminals. Have the post office hold your mail, have newspapers suspended, and have a neighbor or friend clear away flyers.

- Don't leave valuables in sight through windows, where they will tempt burglars. Use an etching pen to mark an ID number, like your driver's license number, on valuables.

- Make an inventory of valuables in your house and store it somewhere other than your home, such as in a safe deposit box.

- Leave curtains slightly parted so your house doesn't have an empty look.

- Never open the door to a stranger. Install peepholes in all exterior doors so you can identify whoever is outside. Do not rely on a door safety chain, because these can be broken easily.

- Ask for identification from service representatives who come to your home, and if they don't have it, check with their company to verify their identity before letting them inside.

- If you are planning to go away, be careful whom you tell about your plans.

- Thieves always look in mailboxes, under doormats, and above doorways for keys. Don't make it easy for them to get into your home.

- Do not put your name or address on your key ring, because it might lead a thief right to your door with key in hand.

- When having a car parked or serviced, leave only the car keys, not your housekeys.

—Adapted from ADT Security Services Information.
See http://www.adt.com/divisions/residential/index.cfm for more info.

- Light up! A dark apartment is an invitation to burglars. Leave on doorway lights and a light or two inside (never leave torchieres on, though—they are a fire hazard).
- Hide. If you are home alone and hear someone breaking in, the best thing to do is get out! If you can't, grab the phone, lock yourself in a room, and call 911 or the police.
- Have emergency numbers by the phone if your area doesn't have 911.
- Move up. Upper floors are generally less vulnerable to break-ins, because you only have to worry about making your front door and your balcony door safe. Burglars are not as likely to crawl through windows if the windows are not at ground level (although thieves have certainly used ladders to gain entry to upper-level apartments).
- Open your eyes. Peepholes don't do you any good if you don't use them.

Safety at School

Keeping yourself safe at school is most often a case of making yourself unavailable to attackers or harassers. Most problems occur in unsupervised areas—the bathrooms, the locker room, or the parking lot.

Whether you are in high school or in college, these are some good common-sense safety tips:

- Go in pairs. Ask a friend or someone from your class to stop by the bathroom with you or walk out to your car with you. If you must walk out to your car alone after dark, ask the school if a security guard can escort you.
- Trust your instincts. If you walk into a bathroom and a group of girls who have harassed you before or who you think are bad news are there, turn around and walk back out. Who cares if they think you are chicken? If there are four of them and one of you, you're putting yourself in a bad situation by staying in there.
- If someone harasses you—physically or sexually—talk to a teacher. If a teacher harasses you, talk to someone at the front office. Try to be angry, not embarrassed. This is not your fault. It is someone else behaving in a totally inappropriate way. Stand up for yourself so that you can keep yourself and others safe.
- Parking lots and deserted paths are some of the most dangerous areas at school, especially after dark. Try not to walk alone to your car or dorm room. When you are walking outside at night, have your keys in one hand and your pepper spray and or rape alarm in the other. Keeping them in your purse does no good. Try to park under lights, and check to make sure your car (which is, of course, locked) is empty before you get in.

Date Rape

Date rape is when a person on a date or in a social situation with someone else forces that person to have sex with them. Date rape is almost always committed by men against women, and its effects are devastating. In addition to the normal range of reactions to rape—anger, sadness, fear, and helplessness—victims of date rape also often feel guilty that they misjudged someone's character. Here are some tips to avoid date rape:

- Watch who you agree to go out alone with. If you don't know someone really well (like having a long history of friendship, working together, or going to school together for a long time), then you should be cautious. Meet at public places the first few times you get together. If he picks you up in his car, you are at his mercy, with no way to get home if things go bad.

- Watch your drink. At parties, get your own drinks, and don't leave them unattended. Same thing on dates. It only takes a few seconds for someone to dissolve a rohypnol tablet, a roofie, in your drink. Roofies are odorless and tasteless, and you won't notice a thing. If you wake up six hours later naked in someone else's house, you might not remember what happened. I don't want to sound paranoid, but roofies are a cheap, easy way to incapacitate a date. They are low-risk, too. Victims often cannot remember enough to prosecute their attackers.

Definitions

Roofie is short for Rohypnol, the brand name of the drug fluni-trazepam. It is a tranquilizer that has become known as the date-rape drug. It is also called rope, mind eraser, Roche, R-2, and roach-2, among other nicknames. This tasteless drug is easily dissolved in drinks and acts quickly, within half an hour. It makes a person drowsy and confused, and they often blank out, losing their memory of the events of several hours. GHB (gamma-hydroxybutyrate) is another drug with similar effects.

- Be assertive. Let your date know where your boundaries are. In an age where many people expect sex on the first date and others don't even want to kiss until the fourth or fifth date, it helps to be very clear at the beginning of the date, especially if you are closer to the no-kissing-right-away end of the spectrum. This is especially important if you do not know the other person well. He or she may still believe that dinner and a movie "earns" him or her sex. It may be uncomfortable to be blunt when you are just getting to know someone, but it's the safest way to go.
- Practice. By yourself, practice saying no to a date's sexual advances. Give your date different reactions, and try to come up with calm responses. When you say no, your date might be angry, embarrassed, or hurt. Practice defusing a hostile situation, and the words will come more easily when you need them.
- Say no! Say it loud, clear, and often. Scream it if he doesn't listen. If you say no and he tries to change your mind, ignores you, or tries to get you drunk or high, he's on the road to raping you. Get out of there as fast as you can.
- Carry a cell phone. Cell phones are great safety devices. If your area doesn't have 911, put the police emergency number into the memory.
- Let your roommate know where you are going and when you will be back. I know, you might have moved out of the house to get away from that kind of stuff. But this isn't to get control over you, it is to help you stay safe and protect yourself from others who want to control you. That way, if you planned to be home by 10 P.M. and you're not home at midnight, your roommate can start checking to make sure you are safe.
- Carry a rape siren or pepper spray. Keep it handy. If your cell phone and your weapon are in your purse, all your date has to do is toss your purse out the window. If possible, keep them in a pocket.
- Go for soft tissue. Fighting back is a personal decision depending on your personality, the setting, and how much danger you feel you are in. If you must fight off

an attacker, go for the eyeballs. They're easier to get to than the testicles. Use your fingers or car keys—whatever you have handy, and hit hard. Then get out of there.

- Don't go too far from home on your first few dates. Stick with settings that you're comfortable with and that you know your way home from.

- Carry cash for a taxi. Put a taxi company's phone number in your cell phone memory, too, in case you are stuck somewhere with no pay phone or phone book.

- Take a self-defense class. If you think it would help you feel less intimidated, take a class to learn some basic self-defense moves. YMCAs, community centers, and schools often offer basic, one- or two-night classes. Sign up with a friend and feel your confidence soar.

By the Numbers

Date rape is the most common kind of rape, accounting for 78% of all reported rapes. Almost 25% of girls will be victims of rape or attempted rape by the time they turn 25. A girl is four times as likely to be raped by someone she knows than by a stranger.

Identity Theft

You have heard about identity theft and wondered if it matters to you. In fact, when things are going bad, you might wish someone would steal your identity! Still, more than 1 million people are victims of identity theft every year, and it is a lot of work to get everything sorted out. It's expensive, too. Here are a few tips to protect other people from using your credit cards, name, and bank accounts for their own good:

- Don't give out your social security number to anyone but your job or school, and don't carry your card with you.

- Put passwords on all the credit cards, e-mail accounts, and other accounts, that you can. It helps to have a standard username and password that you use all the time so that you don't get them mixed up.

- Keep track of your bills. If you don't receive a credit card bill one month, call them up. Someone may have called to change your mailing address, and now they can run up big expenses without your noticing.

General Safety

A few other things to consider for safety. Wherever you spend a fair amount of time—home, school, work—you should know what the emergency procedure is. If a tornado is coming or the civil defense sirens go off, do you know where to go to be safe? You should, so ask the person in charge.

Walking alone in the dark is always a bad idea. Always try to walk with a buddy or a group. Guys are much safer walking alone than girls are, but guys are still not completely safe. Carry your keys and your pepper spray. Walk tall and make eye contact with people. Look tough. Don't look like you would give in to anything without a fight. Most criminals are looking for an easy target, so don't be one.

Resources

Websites

About.com Teen Advice
http://teenadvice.about.com/library/bl10thingsdaterape.htm
A top 10 fact sheet on date rape.

ADT Home Security Systems
http://www.adt.com/divisions/residential/index.cfm
This website has some good tips in its "Powerline/Safe & Sound" section.

Child Labor Coalition
http://www.stopchildlabor.org/
This website provides facts about teen safety on the job.

Equal Employment Opportunity Commission
http://www.eeoc.gov/facts/howtofil.html
This site tells you how to file a sexual harassment charge. You can also call
1-800-669-4000 to file a sexual harassment grievance.
http://www.eeoc.gov/facts/fs-sex.html
This site gives you facts about sexual harassment.

Federal Trade Commission
http://www.consumer.gov/idtheft/index.html
This website has identity theft information.

National Institute for Occupational Safety and Health
http://www.cdc.gov/niosh/homepage.html
Contact this organization with questions or concerns about job safety. You
can also call 1-800-35-NIOSH (1-800-356-4674).

CHAPTER 11

The Commitment

Keeping Up with Your Responsibilities

our life is about to get a lot more complicated. You are going to have the privilege of controlling your schedule, your schooling, and your workload. But as you have probably heard too many times to count, with privilege comes responsibility. And it's true.

Now you are the one responsible for making sure you're not scheduled for a morning shift when you have an 8 A.M. biology class. You are the one who must make your dental appointment work around the rest of your schedule. You are the one responsible for proving that you did pay your electric bill on time. Here are the main areas you need to manage to keep your new life running smoothly: your schedule, your time, your stuff, your finances, and your food. As you make basic decisions in each area, jot them down on Worksheet 8.

Managing Your Schedule

The best way for you to keep track of your time is to put all of your scheduling information in one place. One option is a PDA, a personal digital assistant. This is the generic name for a Palm Pilot or some similar doohickey. It is a small electronic calendar that allows you to store your daily, weekly, and monthly schedule, phone numbers, and a to-do list all in one handy spot.

One good thing about PDAs is that they are portable, so that you can always have yours available. They are also handy because they are not that big for the amount of information you can store on them. They are also convenient for entering standing schedules. For example, if you have school every Monday from 9 A.M. to 2 P.M., you can enter it for the first day of that class on your PDA and then choose to repeat it every week. That way, you don't have to keep reentering the same information. Also, if your plans change a lot, your PDA will not fill up with scribbles and white-outs; you simply delete events.

Worksheet 8

My Plan for Keeping Track of Things

* I'm going to keep track of my schedule (where and in what format?):

  _____

* I plan to keep my household files in:

  _____

* Every day, my keys will go:

  _____

* I am keeping my coaching team list of names, addresses, and phone numbers (where?):

  _____

* I am going to pay bills every:

  _____

* The person I will ask when I have financial or tax questions is:

  _____

* I do / do not plan to make a menu each week. (Circle one.)

* I will keep my grocery list (where—on the fridge, in your calendar?):

  _____

The bad thing about PDAs is that they are a bit pricey, around $100 for a low-end one. I was unsure whether they were worth it, but I got one for Christmas a couple of years ago, and now I couldn't do without it. They are also intimidating for people who don't get computers, but not many teens fit that category!

Another option is a personal calendar. This is a portable paper calendar that has different components available to meet your needs. It is in a small binder, and you choose daily sheets, monthly calendar sheets, phone and address sheets, and so on. At-A-Glance and Day-Runner are just two of many available brands.

The good thing about calendars is that you can keep all sorts of information in them, from budgeting notes, homework sections, daily to-do lists, and so on. They are good for people who like to see things spread out and look at the big picture. The bad thing is that they can get pretty bulky and heavy. For guys, especially, they can be a pain to carry around. For girls, they can fill up a purse fast. You also have to enter a lot of information in a fairly small space. Buying the binder and the refills can get pricey eventually.

One more option is a big wall or desk calendar. This is a calendar big enough to write down everything you need on it. It's hard to lose wall calendars, unlike more portable options, and they are pretty cheap—generally $20 or less for a yearly calendar.

The down side is that you will not have your schedule with you when you're not home. This means a lot of "I'm not sure, let me check my schedule and get back to you," which means more phone calls and hassles. It also means you will still have to carry scraps of paper around with you with information about your coaching team, your grocery list, your emergency phone numbers, or whatever.

Whichever option you choose, try to pick one and stick with it. If you have schedules written in different spots, you might note an appointment on one of them and not the other. This is going to end up with missed appointments and people ticked off at you. Being independent means showing up on time for appointments, classes, work, and dates. It also means turning things in on time, like bills, tax forms, and thesis papers. Keeping a calendar of some kind will help you do all that.

Managing Your Time

This is a huge topic that people have written entire books about. I would just like to share a few tips that work for me to keep me from wasting too much time. I hope some of them will work for you, too:

- Limit your e-mail and Web browsing. Use Internet time as a reward for getting your other stuff done. Otherwise, you can fritter away an hour without even realizing it.

- Work first, play later. This relates to the previous point. In general, take care of your responsibilities first, such as homework and paying bills, and then relax, call a friend, and just hang out. If you do them in reverse order, you might never get to the things that need to be done.

- Break it down. If you have a big project to do, break it down into smaller sections. Give yourself little deadlines. For example, "I will find five sources for my psychology paper by this Friday." Jot those minideadlines down on your calendar.

- Learn to say no. Of course, you want to be a good neighbor and help out other people sometimes, just as you will need them to help you, however, you can't always give rides to people or help them study or you won't get your own stuff done. Likewise, you won't be able to always say yes to social invitations, even though they sound good. Look at your calendar and really think about it before you agree to anything. Think about all the things you need to do that aren't on your calendar, too, like cleaning the litter box and stopping by the library. Then answer yes or no.

- Use your voicemail or answering machine. When you are working on schoolwork or household stuff that you need to concentrate on, don't answer the phone. Let it ring. It won't kill you. Once you finish what you're working on, you can check messages and call people back.

- If people often drop by, and you can't ignore the phone, doorbell, and e-mail, leave the house for a while. Take your checkbook and your pile of bills to the library or a Burger King or whatever, and work or study here. Sometimes our "private" home just lets too many other people interrupt us and it is actually easier to tune strangers out in a public place!

You might have noticed that a lot of these involve distractions and interruptions. So much of the time, we don't get our stuff done because something else comes along and we get caught up in it. By making a more purposeful effort to focus on what you are supposed to be doing, you'll get more done in less time.

Organizing Your Place

I'm no Martha Stewart. I'm not going to tell you how to color code your towels and make marzipan roses for your table. But I will tell you that being disorganized wastes a lot of your time and money. I should know—I've spent hours looking for bills I should have paid, letters I should have answered, and homework I should have turned in. I've also spent plenty of money I worked pretty hard for to buy stuff I already have but can't find. Very irritating!

So, here's my suggestion. Buy a cheap filing cabinet or a couple of filing crates and a couple of boxes of hanging folders. Then, create all the files you need to keep track of stuff.

For instance, you'll want a file for each company that regularly sends you a bill: electric company, water company, cable, Internet access, phone, and so on. You will also need a file for bills to pay and a file for your lease and any apartment or housing issues. Other possible files might include insurance (both auto and health), pet information, vehicle papers, bank statements, and taxes. Saving up for a weekend trip to the beach? Start a file on it. Working on Christmas lists for your family? Start a file.

Then, whenever you have a piece of paper relating to that topic, dump it into the file. It's that simple. If a question comes up such as, How much was that hotel you were going to stay at? you'll know where to find the answer. If your cable provider says you didn't pay the bill, you will know where to find the last bill with your payment info on it.

If you are attending school, you might want a whole separate drawer or crate just for school stuff. You might need a financial aid file, a file for each class you're taking, a file with information about the major you are pursuing, and a file with the academic calendar in it. Have a big paper coming due? Start a file for it and keep your drafts in it as you work on it.

Following this one simple suggestion will make your household run so much more smoothly. I also like to keep a bunch of blank files at the back of the drawer so that when I need a new one, I just pull one to the front, fill out the little paper tab, and I'm ready to go. Otherwise, those papers go into a "need a file" pile and I never see them again.

Here are a few other basic hints for keeping your place organized enough to be able to enjoy it:

- Box up stuff you don't use often or year-round. Write the contents (winter coat and long johns, my report cards from 1st–12th grade, Hanukkah decorations) on the side of the box and store it somewhere out of the way with the contents list showing. Stow it on that top closet shelf you can't reach very well, or in an under-bed box. Make sure to keep the list of contents up to date so that you don't have to pull out and open 15 boxes to find that 9th-grade yearbook you want to show someone.

- Keep stuff where you use it. Pretty simple. Store kitchen-related stuff in the kitchen, if at all possible. Keeping your box of mittens and ear muffs on the top kitchen shelf and your make-a-pizza kit in your bedroom closet doesn't make much sense.

- Always keep stuff in the same place. Have a spot where you dump your keys every time you come in the door. That will save you lots of mornings of frantically going through last night's clothes, piles of mail, and other stuff trying to get out of the house on time.

Paying Bills and Filing Taxes

One of your new responsibilities is paying bills. It's important to pay your bills on time so that you start building up a good credit rating, and also so that your electricity or cable doesn't get turned off!

There are lots of ways to pay your bills. Because many jobs for teens have weekly paychecks, I think paying bills on a weekly basis makes sense. If you want to do this, pick a day to take care of it every week. It is easier to remember if you just get into the habit of saying, "Oh, it's Tuesday (or Monday, or Wednesday, or whatever), gotta pay bills."

You dump out your bills-to-pay file on the table and get out your checkbook. Now, say today is the 8th. You get paid tomorrow, the 9th. You won't pay bills again until next

Tuesday, the 15th. It can take mail up to four days to get where it needs to go in the United States, so add four days to the 15th–that's the 19th. Therefore, today, on the 8th, you should be paying all bills that are due on the 19th or earlier.

Go through the bills you just dumped out on the table, find the ones due the 19th or before, and set them aside. Put the rest of the bills back in the bills-to-pay file and put it back in your filing crate.

By the Numbers

You could easily have 12 to 15 monthly bills to pay. By paying weekly, you will probably only need to process three or four bills per week. If you start losing track, though, they will quickly snowball and you can be buried under an avalanche of overdue notices.

Open your first bill. Look it over and make sure that it appears to be correct. If so, write your check and tear off the portion of the bill to include with your check. Put them both in the envelope and seal it. Make sure the company's address is showing through the window box, if it's that kind of envelope, before you seal it.

On the part of the bill you keep, write down the date you paid it, the amount you paid, and the check number you paid it with. If the bill has more than one page, staple the pages together. Then, drop the bill into the correct file (electricity, cable, etc.). Last, enter the check information in your checkbook register.

Do that with each bill in the pile. Stamp them all and write your return address on them. Now they are ready to mail and you are done for the week. Simple.

If you don't agree with the amount you've been billed for something, call the billing inquiries number listed on the bill and discuss it with someone.

That's pretty much all there is to paying bills. It doesn't need to be a big deal. If you keep bills scattered all over the apartment, don't pay them on time, and don't keep track of when you paid them, however, you will find out quickly that that *is* a big deal.

Taxes

As far as taxes go, if you are earning enough money to live off, then you will be paying taxes, too. Maybe for the first time in your life.

Each January, your employer will send you a W-2 form that shows how much you made, the amounts of federal and state taxes deducted from your pay, and other information. If you don't receive a tax booklet in the mail from the IRS, stop by a post office or library and pick up a 1040 form and a 1040 EZ form and directions. Read the directions to see which form you need to fill out. You can also download forms directly from the IRS website. You can file your taxes anytime between January 1st and April 15th.

If you have questions about how to fill out your taxes, call your local library or your school and ask if they have any service available to help young people fill out taxes. Otherwise, check with an adult you know and trust, someone from your coaching team.

Withholding Allowances

When you begin a new job, your employer will have you fill out a W-4 form. On this form, you certify that you are a U.S. citizen and you give your legal name, address, and so on. You also make decisions that affect the amount of taxes withheld from your paychecks. If you check single (assuming you are single) and just one withholding on your W-4, theoretically, at tax time, you will neither owe money nor get a refund.

But you might choose to claim zero withholding allowances (rather than the technically correct "one") on your W-4 form, however, or fill out an amount like $10 or $25 on the line that says, "Additional amount, if any, you want withheld from each paycheck." If you do this, IRS will deduct more taxes from your paycheck each week throughout the year. But at tax time next year, you will be more likely to qualify for a refund. That chunk of a few hundred dollars is spring break vacation money for teens all over the country!

Financial advisors will tell you that this is not a smart way to save money, but for some teens...okay, for me, too, still...it works.

The IRS website, http://www.irs.gov/index.html, has tutorials on filling out a W-4 form, filing taxes, and more. called TAX Interactive. Check out the help page to get IRS's answers to your tax questions.

How to Get People to Take You Seriously

It might be when you call about your checking account. Or when you are filling out financial aid forms. Or when you shop for a car. But sooner or later, someone is going to say, "You need to have your mom or dad call us." In other words, they are used to dealing with adults about this stuff, and they are not sure if you are really responsible for yourself.

What do you say? You will probably want to have a little spiel all ready. "I don't live with my parents. I'm completely self-supporting and am working full-time and trying to get this [whatever you're talking with the person about] taken care of. What do you think my next step should be?"

With a statement like this, you'll come across as responsible and mature, but not snotty. Hopefully, the person to whom you are speaking will either take care of what you need help with or will tell you who you need to speak with to get it taken care of.

You don't need to spill your guts to people. Most people just need the bare bones information: You do not have any adults running your life, and you need to figure out

---

Things You Might Need to Know

- Are you an emancipated minor?

- Did your parents claim you as a deduction on last year's taxes?

- What adults can vouch for you? (Have your coaching team list handy.)

- What was your taxable income (if any) last year?

- What's your monthly income now?

- What's your estimated income for this year?

Phone Calls

Maybe you already like talking on the phone. That's good preparation for independent living, because you will have to make an amazing number of phone calls, especially when you deal with the government on any level, such as for social work and independent living resources.

A few tips for the phone calls you make, whether they are to the financial aid office, the trash collection company, or the university's admission office:

- Don't call if you only have five minutes. You'll wait on hold that long or longer for many offices.

- Take notes during the call, and include the date and the name of the person you spoke to. Then drop the notes in the appropriate file in your file crate.

- Have the facts in front of you. If you are calling to complain about a bill, have the bill there in front of you, so that you can answer their questions.

- Get used to it. You will make lots of phone calls and repeat the same information to lots of people, many of whom won't be the right ones to help you. It's good to know that going in, to try to keep your frustration level down.

- Use e-mail when possible. Sometimes, you'll be able to use e-mail. Many social service organizations, medical providers, and schools, however, will not use e-mail because of confidentiality concerns. But it doesn't hurt to ask!

how to do things yourself. You don't need to tell them that you were abused, or that you ran away, or that your parents were so unfair. You don't need to tell them how hard you're working, how psyched you are to get to do whatever you want, or anything like that.

Your personal information is your own. You should not have to parade your personal miseries in front of people to get help or cooperation, even if you are younger than the people they generally deal with.

The exception to this rule is if you are talking to people in agencies or organizations that might provide you with services or financial aid. You may well need to justify why you are in need of certain services, so don't hold back on your fears, worries, and needs when you talk to them.

Feeding Yourself: Where Do You Start?

If you have no idea what to put on a menu or a grocery list, then you have probably relied on school lunches and parents to feed you the last several years. That's okay—you don't have to be a gourmet to feed yourself. Check out the several great cookbooks geared for beginning cooks in the resources section at the end of this chapter.

Making a Menu

The best way to make sure you have decent, fast, cheap meals is to make a menu. It's pretty simple, really. You just use the grid chart to fill in the meals you will eat this week.

The main thing is to try to be realistic. If you have class until 4 p.m., and you have to be at work at 5:30, that is not the night to prepare roasted chicken with vegetables for dinner; that's a night for a quick microwave meal or a sandwich, or running through a fast-food place.

Check out the sample menu I've included on the next page. Copy Worksheet 9 and fill it out for the coming week.

Remember, this is not to restrict you. If you wrote microwave pizza on Monday, but come Monday, you really feel more like the chicken salad sandwich you wrote down for Wednesday, fine. The menu police won't come beating down your door. Just make sure you leave yourself options for the really rushed meal times or those times when you are not going to be at home. In other words, if you were planning to take that sandwich in an insulated lunch bag to eat on your work break, a microwave pizza isn't going to fit well there.

Grocery Shopping

Basically, grocery shopping stinks. You've got the crowds, the lines, the cost. I know a few people who enjoy it, but I'm pretty sure there's something wrong with them! Here's the deal. Your cooking will be easier with a menu, and your shopping will be easier with a list, and cheaper, too.

So, look at your menu for this week's meals. If your chart says cereal for breakfast every day, fine. Check your pantry. Is there enough cereal for seven breakfasts? Yes? You're all set. No? Add a box to your list. I like to make the list right on the back of the menu, but that's up to you.

That's about it. Once you have the ingredients for all your meals on your list, think about what else you might need. Snacks for home? Portable snacks for your backpack? Toilet paper, paper towels, deodorant? Dog food, toothpaste? Note that household and paper items are usually less expensive at big discount stores, such as Target and Wal-Mart, than they are at grocery stores, so you might want to make a separate trip to buy them somewhere else.

Sample Weekly Menu

DAY	BREAKFAST	LUNCH	DINNER
Monday	Cereal with milk; banana	Sandwich: turkey, lettuce, cheese; baked chips; orange juice	Caribbean Rice and Ham (freeze leftovers); salad
Tuesday	Peanut butter on toast; milk, banana	Fast food with Terry, burger and side salad?	Tacos (freeze leftovers): meat, cheese, lettuce, tomatoes; fruit cocktail
Wednesday	Cereal with milk; apple	Nachos with leftover taco meat; juice	Cowboy Stew (freeze leftovers); biscuits; canned peaches
Thursday	Peanut butter on toast; milk; apple	Lunch at Student Center Cafe	Leftover Caribbean Rice and Ham; salad
Friday	Cereal with milk; yogurt	Taco salad; juice	Microwave pizza
Saturday	Scrambled cheesy eggs; orange juice	Sandwich: turkey, lettuce, cheese; yogurt	Pasta Alfredo for One; broccoli
Sunday	Cold Fruit Cereal; orange juice; sausage links	Watch the game with group: Bring chips with South of Border Dip and Chocolate Chip Wedges	Cowboy Stew leftovers; salad; breadsticks

Worksheet 9

Weekly Menu

DAY	BREAKFAST	LUNCH	DINNER
Monday			
Tuesday			
Wednesday			
Thursday			
Friday			
Saturday			
Sunday			

Expert Advice: A Dozen Grocery Dollar Stretchers

Groceries are one of the few items in your monthly budget that can be at least a little bit flexible, however, it can be challenging to find creative ways to save on regular food costs. The following are some simple tips for reducing your grocery expenses:

1. Plan ahead by making out your shopping list in advance. It helps to know what you're going to eat, and when. With fewer last minute food-related decisions, this also helps keep you away from developing a first-name relationship with the pizza delivery guy.

2. Set your grocery budget and then make sure your menu and grocery list fit your budget. Don't plan on eating chicken cordon bleu if your budget only allows for rice and beans. And don't let yourself give into a pity party, thinking, "I can only eat rice and beans tonight. Boo hoo!" Rice and beans are good food! Just think how healthy you (and your budget!) will be.

3. Plan your meals around items you already have on hand in your cupboards and refrigerator, and around the sale flyers from your local grocery stores.

4. Do your grocery shopping with cash. This is a surprisingly easy way of staying within your budget. Keep a running total of how much you're spending at the store. If you find you're about to spend more than you had budgeted for that trip, put items back and shop for better bargains.

5. A simple rule of thumb when you're shopping is: "Look high, look low." Stores often place the most expensive items at eye level.

6. Stores often place their advertised specials at the end of aisles. The advertised special might be a good buy, but the item will often be displayed with non-sale (and very expensive!) products to lure you into impulse purchases.

7. Check store entrances or bulletin boards for special flyers and coupon specials, and don't forget to look in local newspapers for additional coupons. Only use coupons for those items and brands that you would normally purchase. And always check the expiration date on your coupons. Some stores offer double coupons—check with your favorite store and see if they do. Some stores will even accept competitor's coupons. Hand your coupons to the cashier before they start to ring up your order so you don't forget later.

8. Stock up on frequently used items when they go on sale (canned goods, toilet paper, shampoo, etc.).

9. Only stock up on items you know you'll use before they go bad. Stockpiling toilet paper is a good idea, but bananas might be another story.

10. Natural food co-ops are becoming quite common. This can be a great way to purchase organic fruits and vegetables, whole grains, and other usually expensive items at lower prices.

11. Watch for sales on lean ground meats. Divide the meat into one-pound batches and then freeze in individual zip-top freezer bags.

12. Don't shop when you're hungry. You're more liable to make impulse buys when your stomach's rumbling.

—*Deborah Taylor-Hough* is the author of *Frozen Assets: How to Cook for a Day and Eat for a Month* and *Frugal Living for Dummies*®. Visit her online at http://www.simplemom.com.

Before you leave for the store, clear out your fridge. Now is the time to get rid of leftovers you're not going to eat, that last cracked, dried-out piece of Swiss cheese, and anything fuzzy.

At the grocery store, start with the dry food aisles. That's everything room temperature in a can, a box, or a bag on the shelves in the main part of the store. I like to cross off each item as I buy it. Then take care of frozen goods, produce, dairy, and meat. That way, your milk and ground beef won't sit in your cart growing bacteria while you shop for an hour.

I try to zip around the store as quickly as possible. The longer you stare at your options, the more likely you are to buy a lot of snack and convenience foods that are not on your list. Remember also that bigger food containers aren't a bargain if you throw half of the food out. So what if the 28-ounce can of tomato sauce is 54 cents and the 14-ounce is 50 cents? Theoretically, the bigger size is the better deal. But why pay 4 cents for 14 ounces of tomato sauce to pour down the sink?

Six Great Easy-to-Cook Meals

There are many cookbooks geared toward people with not much time, money, or desire to cook. Here are a few recipes to try.

Cold Fruit Cereal
Makes 2 servings.

1/4 cup uncooked quick oats

1/2 cup skim milk

1/4 cup plain nonfat yogurt

1/2 cup orange juice

1 1/2 tablespoons honey

1 chopped apple

1/4 cup mixed fruit, chopped *(optional)*

In a medium bowl, combine the oats, milk, and yogurt. Let stand for five minutes to allow the oats to soften. Stir in the orange juice, honey, apples, and mixed fruit. Mix well. Serve cold.

Note: Recipe excerpted from the book *The healthy college cookbook*. Copyright 1999 by Alexandra Nimetz, Jason Stanley, and Emeline Starr. Used with permission from the publisher, Storey Publishing, LLC.

Pasta Alfredo for One
Makes 1 serving.

Instead of traditional fettuccine, use noodles. Cook two handfuls of medium egg noodles for 10 minutes. Drain them and return them to saucepan. Over medium-high heat, add a small lump of butter to the noodles and sprinkle with black pepper. Stir for a minute. Drizzle a few tablespoons of light cream (15% or half-and-half) on top, sprinkle with grated Parmesan cheese, and stir until hot and creamy, for 2 to 3 minutes. Eat immediately.

Note: Adapted from Peltosaari, L. (1998). *College cuisine*. Quebec, Canada: Tikka Books.

Caribbean Rice and Ham
Makes 4 servings. Easy to make in large quantity for a crowd.

2 cups water

1/2 tsp salt

1 cup uncooked long-grain rice

1 cup shredded ham

1 cup shredded cheese (*Gruyere or old cheddar*)

1 14-oz. can pineapple tidbits

Pinch of cayenne pepper

In medium saucepan, bring water to boil. Add salt and rice. Stir once. Reduce heat to minimum; cover and simmer for 17 minutes. Uncover and fluff the rice with fork. Stir ham, cheese, and pineapple into hot rice, and add some of the pineapple juice. Stir. Sprinkle lightly with cayenne pepper.

Note: Adapted from Peltosaari, L. (1998). *College cuisine*. Quebec, Canada: Tikka Books.

South of the Border Chip Dip

Makes 8 servings.

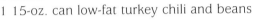

1 16-oz. can fat-free refried beans

1 cup low-fat sour cream

1 tablespoon taco seasoning

1 cup salsa

1 cup shredded low-fat cheddar cheese

1 tomato, diced

1/4 cup fresh cilantro leaves (optional)

Spread the beans evenly in a small casserole dish to form the bottom layer of the dip. Mix together the sour cream and taco seasoning and then spread evenly over the beans. Top with the salsa. Spread the cheese, tomato, and cilantro evenly over the salsa. Serve with tortilla chips as a party food.

Note: Recipe excerpted from the book *The healthy college cookbook*. Copyright 1999 by Alexandra Nimetz, Jason Stanley, and Emeline Starr. Used with permission from the publisher, Storey Publishing, LLC.

Cowboy Stew

Makes 4 servings.

1 15-oz. can low-fat turkey chili and beans

1 lb. extra-lean ground beef

14-oz. can original or barbecue flavor baked beans

1 onion, chopped

1/4 cup shredded reduced-fat Cheddar cheese

In a large nonstick pan, brown the beef and the onion. Drain the grease. Dump in the chili and beans. Simmer for 30 minutes. Toss on the cheese.

Note: Used with permission from *A man, a can, a plan: 50 great guy meals even you can make*. Rodale Books, available wherever books are sold or from www.rodale.com.

Chocolate Chip Wedges

Makes 1 to 4 servings.

1/4 cup (1/2 stick) butter or margarine

1/2 cup sugar

1/2 cup light or dark brown sugar

1 large egg

1 cup flour

1 teaspoon baking powder

1/2 teaspoon salt

1/2 teaspoon vanilla extract

1 cup *(6-ounce package)* semisweet chocolate chips

Place one of the oven racks in the middle position, and preheat the oven to 350°F. To save time on cleaning up, I cook and bake in the same container. Place a metal— not glass—pie pan on a stove burner over low heat. Melt the butter or margarine right in the pan. As soon as it is melted, turn off the heat. Add the sugar and brown sugar and stir thoroughly. Add the egg, vanilla, flour, baking powder, and salt and stir until they are well combined. Mix in the chocolate chips, making sure they are well distributed through the batter. Bake for 30 minutes, or until the top browns and begins to pull away from the sides of the pan. Cool on a rack. Serve cut into thin wedges. Or you can cut it into any shapes you want: squares, figure-8s, and so on.

Note: Adapted with permission from Mills, K., & Mills, N. (1996). *Help! My apartment has a kitchen: 100 + great recipes with foolproof instruction*. New York: Houghton Mifflin. All rights reserved.

Resources

Books

Beverly, S. (1998). *The kitchenless cookbook*. Davie, FL: InterMedia.
> If you have a microwave, a blender, and nothing else, this cookbook is for you. It gives you menus, shopping lists, and 124 simple recipes. $21.95. Most recipes serve one or two, although some party dishes are included, too.

Joachim, D., & the editors of *Men's Health*. (2002). *A man,. a can, a plan: 50 great guy meals even you can make*. New York: Rodale Books.
> These simple recipes rely heavily on canned and prepackaged foods.

Mills, K., & Mills, N. (1996). *Help! My apartment has a kitchen: 100 + great recipes with foolproof instruction*. New York: Houghton Mifflin.
> This cookbook features recipes for lots of very basic dishes. A lot of short ingredient lists and "Mom Tips," along with very explicit directions, make this a good choice for beginners. $17.

Morgenstern, J., & Morgenstern-Colón, J. (2002). *Organizing from the inside out for teenagers*. New York: Owl Books.

Nimetz, A., Stanley, J., & Starr, E. (1999). *The healthy college cookbook*. Pownal, VT: Storey.
> This cookbook offers recipes for every meal, plus snacks and desserts. It emphasizes simple recipes for healthy foods and includes nutritional information for every recipe. $14.95.

Peltosaari, L. (1998). *College cuisine*. Quebec, Canada: Tikka Books.
> This great little cookbook (spiral-bound to lay flat on your kitchen countertop) focuses on easy, inexpensive recipes. Includes recipes for one, crowd pleasers, ways to use up leftover ingredients, and recipes for every meal of the day. Order from P.O. Box 203, Chambly, Quebec J3L 4B3, Canada; 450/658-6205; or http://www.tikkabooks.com. $9.95 in bookstores, or order it directly from the above address for $8, including shipping.

Taylor-Hough, D. (1998). *Frozen assets: How to cook for a day and eat for a month*. Beverly Hills, CA: Champion Press.
> This cookbook is full of recipes you can fix and freeze in individual servings, even if you do not want to do a month's worth of cooking at once.

Taylor-Hough, D. (2001). *Frozen assets lite and easy : How to cook for a day and eat for a month*. Beverly Hills, CA: Champion Press.
> This fix and freeze cookbook focuses on nutritious recipes.

Hotlines

Internal Revenue Service Telephone Assistance
> 1-800-829-1040
>
> This hotline has live people during tax season (January through April) and has recorded messages on various tax topics the rest of the year.

Internal Revenue Service Tele-Tax Recorded Tax Info
> 1-800-829-4477

Websites

Internal Revenue Service
> http://www.irs.gov/index.html
>
> Download forms and instructions, learn how to fill out forms, and ask for help.

Recipe Source
> http://www.recipesource.com/
>
> This is an online searchable recipe guide.

Simple Mom
> http://www.simplemom.com
>
> This website has tips for living a more purposeful and less expensive life.

CHAPTER *12*

Freestyle
Finally, Time for Fun

For this entire book, I have been telling you about all the things you have to do to be independent, how hard it is, how much responsibility you will have, and so on. So, here's the good news: As an independent person, you are in charge of what you get to do for fun. You don't have a curfew, you don't have a time limit on your phone calls or your TV watching, and you don't have to finish your homework before you go out with your friends. You still need to make legal, responsible choices, of course, but the key here is that they are *your* choices.

What Do You Want to Do?

What are you passionate about? Do you love to go dancing? Do you need time to hang out and chat with your friends? Maybe dirt biking or modern art museums do it for you. The key is to find a way to keep the things you love in your life, even when you are busy and broke.

Right now, grab a pencil and write down the last three times you felt totally happy. Maybe they all happened last week, or maybe the most recent one is from two years ago. It doesn't matter. Just write down where you were, what you were doing, and who you were with.

Now, look at each item and decide what was the best thing about that event. Was it where you were, who you were with, or what you were doing? Circle that portion on each line.

Those three circled items need to be things that you keep in your life, if at all possible. If your three circled items are the beach, horseback riding, and your big sister, think about ways to fit those into your life.

Is the beach nearby, or was that on a special vacation? If the beach is within a couple of hours' drive, try to block off one day a month during warm months to pack up the blanket, sunscreen, and a cooler with lunch, and hit the beach.

Horseback riding too expensive for you now? See if you can exchange a morning of mucking out stalls for a couple of hours' worth of riding once or twice a month. Losing touch with your big sister? If she lives locally, call her now and plan to get together once a month. Set the first date now to be sure to hold it open. If she's out of town, set up a specific time for a weekly phone call. Or promise to send each other two postcards per month, looking for the wackiest ones you can find. Just getting that postcard will brighten your whole day.

Quiz

Introvert or Extrovert

Simply put, an introvert is someone who enjoys spending time alone and feels energized after some time by himself or herself. An extrovert is someone who likes to be around other people and recharges his or her battery by conversations with others. Nothing is wrong with either style of personality.

Circle the answers below that are closest to what you would choose.

You are tired of studying and want a break. Do you:

go for a walk or watch a TV show   *OR*   call a friend to see what's up

You have just spent a day downtown with all your friends. Do you feel:

content but exhausted   *OR*   raring to go

You are sick with the flu. Do you:

bury your head in your pillow and sleep   *OR*   call your brother to come over

You have one day off this entire month. Do you:

plan on a movie, and, finally, some alone time   *OR*   make plans for an all-day-into-night blast

At work, do you like to:

focus on your work and chat at lunch   *OR*   talk all day while you get your work done

In class, the teacher asks a question, and you know the answer. Do you:

look at the teacher, hoping she'll pick you   *OR*   raise your hand, murmuring, "I know!"

What Your Score Tells You

If you circled lots of answers on the left side, you are an introvert. Make sure you build some alone time into your schedule. Work and school might make it hard to get any private time, and that could leave you feeling stressed and overwhelmed.

If you circled lots of answers on the right side, you are an extrovert. You might have to be careful not to let your social life get in the way of the commitments you make. Find time for fun, but make sure to get your necessary stuff done first!

The people, places, and activities that are important to you need to remain in your life, but the way they are in your life might have to change. You no longer live with your sister, so you're going to lose touch on some of the little daily things. You have to build a new kind of relationship with her. If the beach is too far away, you're going to look for the biggest lake or swimming hole around and try to recreate the hot, sandy day. Or start a savings envelope for a weekend trip to the beach, even if you have to drive six hours to get there. Basically, you've got to ask yourself, How can I keep this connection with my life as it is right now?

Cheap Entertainment

If you have financial support from someone, a good job, and low costs, then you might be able to afford the things you like to do. For most independent teens, though, your fun is going to have to be very cheap. Here are strategies for having fun without blowing your budget.

- **Exchange privileges.** If you would love to join the YMCA, take a dance class, or learn a new sport, but you can't afford the fees, try this. Call the office or organization and explain that you're interested in a class but you can't afford the fees. Ask if they have any work that needs to be done in exchange. Many organizations will let a limited number of people work a few hours in exchange for free classes. I have volunteered at a YMCA three hours per week in exchange for a free single membership, and I took a 1-1/2 hour dance class I couldn't afford by working the front desk for the hour before my class.
- **Look for free days.** Zoos, museums, parks, history centers, and other places often have at least one free day per month. Call or check out their websites to find out. It is often something like the second Tuesday of every month. You'll find it crowded on those days, as lots of day care centers and people with no extra money take advantage of it. You might want to go extra early or extra late to beat some of the crowds.
- **See some shows.** In larger cities, theaters sometimes open dress rehearsals to the public for free or very low cost. Again, simply call and ask. If they do this, ask if they have a mailing list you can be put on to be notified of these events.
- **Check school and church activities.** Both of these offer low-cost activities and trips, because they are usually not trying to make a profit. If a church or school has something you would like to do but can't afford, call and ask if there are any scholarship funds available. It's simpler than you might think to get a yes.
- **Check the paper.** If you live near a fair-sized city, check the entertainment section. Many papers offer a listing of area events every Friday. These usually list a variety of free or cheap performances and events.
- **Go early.** In general, early is cheaper. Lunch out is less expensive than dinner out. Matinee movies are cheaper. Early comedy shows might be cheaper.
- **Try a festival.** In many areas of the country, festivals are the big thing, especially during summer. Festivals range from Shakespeare festivals with free plays performed in the park to rhubarb festivals selling food I'd think twice about! The nice thing about festivals is that someone else organizes them and invites you. They are lots of fun for people who just want to walk around, chat with friends, and do something different. Pack some food and drinks in your backpack, though, so you don't pay $7 for a hot dog. If you are an impulse buyer,

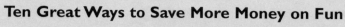

Ten Great Ways to Save More Money on Fun

Everyone wants to have a great time, but no one wants to spend big bucks to do it. Fortunately, a ton of ways to have a great time for free or super-cheap are around. Here are a few of my faves:

1. Usher at concerts. In the last month, I've seen Richard Thompson, Chuck Berry, and Willie Nelson—for free. If I'd paid for tickets it would have cost me about $120 (three different shows)—but I went an hour and a half early and showed people to their seats. Your musical taste might be different—but isn't it nice to see top-name concerts and pay nothing for them?

2. Like to eat out? Go to the tourist info booth and get the restaurant coupons. Usually it's something like 2 for 1, or free dessert. Check it out!

3. Catch the freebies. Colleges, museums, libraries, and parks often have free concerts or plays, free film screenings, and more. Find the events in newspaper calendar listings or get on the mailing lists for these organizations. Check your town's community website, too.

4. Win tickets on the radio. Easy to do on college stations, especially if you program the station's phone number into your speed dial.

5. Volunteer at a radio station. Lots of chances to get freebies—and I'm not talking about stealing, either! (Stealing is a really bad idea—don't do it!)

6. Take your special person out on a hot cheap date: hike a mountain together, rent a rowboat, people watch in a fancy neighborhood, go to the best restaurant in town and just order dessert, fly a kite on an empty beach in winter.

7. Bikes and skateboards are awesome: cost basically nothing to operate, and in crowded cities, they're actually faster than cars. Better for the earth, too.

8. Check out street fairs, art openings, college open houses, trade shows that don't charge admission. You can usually score free food and sometimes all sorts of other goodies (flying toys, umbrellas, pens, CDs, books...).

9. Go to a restaurant together with three friends and agree to share around. Order two main courses and two appetizers. It's probably going to be plenty of food, and way cheaper than buying four entrees.

10. If you like to travel, join a homestay organization or a hostel group and forget the cost of a hotel. (I list 20 different ones in my book.)

—Horowitz, S. (1995). *The Penny-Pinching Hedonist: How to Live Like Royalty with a Peasant's Pocketbook.* Northampton, MA: Accurate Writing & More. This book offers 280 pages of money-saving ideas on how to have fun cheaply. Visit http://www.frugalfun.com and sign up to get a new frugal fun tip in your inbox every month, for free. Mention this article and get $4 off the price of the book.

put the amount of money you've budgeted in your pocket, in cash, and leave the checkbook and credit card in the car or at home.

- **Buy a season's worth.** If there's someplace you love to go that's fairly pricey, look into a season ticket or yearly pass. Community pools, sports teams, and theme parks all offer season or annual tickets. That's not to say they're cheap, but if visiting a theme park is your favorite thing to do, and if you are willing to make it your main entertainment for the season or even for the year, it might be a great deal. This works out especially well if a friend also buys a pass so you have someone to go with on a regular basis.
- **Look for a job that entertains you.** If you love to go to movies, try to get a part-time job as a ticket taker, just for the free movie benefit. Just working a steady one or two nights per week won't make you much money, but the perk of free movies anytime you want will be worth it, if you're a movie fan.

Making New Friends

You know the old saying: Make new friends, but keep the old; one is silver, and the other's gold. It's true. You don't want to lose your old friends when you start a new lifestyle. But the truth is, whether you stay in your hometown or move far away, your life is going to change drastically.

It can be hard explaining to your old friends that you can't afford the $50 night out they have planned. They can use the family car and have no rent to pay. Sometimes they will think you're just being a downer who doesn't like to have fun anymore.

So, make sure to make plans with your old friends, but keep some control over them. Come up with an idea you can afford, then call and invite them along. Or better yet, invite everyone to your place. They can each bring a munchie, and you can rent a great movie to watch, play board games, or just hang out.

You may find that your free time is now all in the morning because of your changed school and work schedules, or that you lose interest in some activities you used to like to do. So you're wondering about making new friends.

Making new friends is not a betrayal of your old friends (unless you suddenly cut your old friends out of your life). It's only natural to want to make some friends who are in a similar situation as you: broke and not living at home anymore. Hanging out at college, joining a group you are interested in, or taking a sports class can all be great ways to meet friends. Just try to be open to other people. Most of all, make your life the fullest it can be by filling it with activities you enjoy. Then the friendships will come along naturally.

Alone Is Not the Same as Lonely

Because you no longer travel in a pack from class to lunch to class to home, you might find that you spend more time alone as you get settled into your new life. If you're not used to that, it can be a little unsettling. But the truth is, being alone can be great. When you are alone, nobody expects anything from you.

If you are going to be eating at a restaurant or the cafeteria by yourself and you're uncomfortable about it, bring along a book or a magazine to read. Remind yourself that other people really couldn't care less what you're doing. They are not whispering, "Look at that poor lonely guy. Nobody to eat with."

At sporting events, concerts, and stuff like that, just nod and smile at the person next to you. If conversation happens, great. If not, so what? You are there to enjoy watching someone else, so it doesn't matter if you're chatting with other people or not. Just cheer, clap, and do whatever you do to get into the show, and don't worry about looking pathetic. You don't. You look confident and independent.

How to Keep Your Old Friends

Sometimes the distance between your new life and your old friends may feel too far to bridge. Here are some simple ways to stay in touch.

- **Keep up your traditions.** If you and your best friend always shop for bathing suits together in March, call her at the end of February and make plans. This gives your relationship continuity and assures your friend that some things won't change.
- **Talk.** Explain how busy you are with work and school, but tell him you still want to hang out, beat him at racquetball, whatever.
- **Set up new routines.** What do you want to do that you aren't finding time for in your new life? Exercise? See if an old buddy wants to jog at 4 P.M. on Wednesdays. Crafts? Set up a date with your sister to work on knitting or Christmas gifts or scrapbooking the third Thursday of each month. By combining a person you want to stay in touch with and an activity you want or need to do, you kill two birds with one stone.
- **Don't expect their lives to change with yours.** Realize that your friends still have curfews, family rules, and old routines to deal with. Just as they shouldn't expect you to have the amount of time and money you used to, you cannot expect them to have the freedom you have. Find a middle ground to enjoy together.
- **Call.** If you don't have time to chat or get together right now, call when you know they are not home. Leave a message: "How was the math test today? Hope you didn't bomb it. I'm swamped with finals, but maybe we can get together in a couple of weeks?"
- **E-mail.** E-mail is the best way to keep in touch, because you can answer it whenever you are awake and have five minutes. You don't have to worry about getting caught up in a long phone call but can still feel connected.

TOP 10 Ten Best Things to Do For Free

1. Take your roller-blades, your Frisbee, your dog, or whatever, and head to the park.
2. Visit a friend or family member you haven't seen in a while.
3. Watch a parade.
4. Go to a reading or performance at a library or bookstore.
5. Play board games.
6. Take a nap.
7. Go window shopping someplace you can't afford to buy anything.
8. If it is holiday time, walk or drive around to check out all the decorations.
9. Spread a blanket out on the grass and read a book you've been wanting to read.
10. Round up friends for a game of softball, football, or old-fashioned kickball.

Getting Married

When you are newly independent and life is an adventure, your passion for another person may make you think that it's time to get married. Or maybe independence is hard and you just think life will be easier if you go ahead and get married now.

Making life easier is no reason to get married. Seriously. If you've moved out of the house to gain independence, then it is time for you to be independent. If you get married because you are afraid you can't make it on your own, then you're just putting yourself in a state of dependence again.

Add to that the fact that 50% of marriages of women younger than 18 end within 15 years. If you really love this person, wait a bit. Make it through school. Get established in a job. Then start a life together. Statistically, your marriage will stand a much better chance of success at that point.

If you want to move in together, that's fine. I'm not trying to give you moral advice. But for your own sake, don't become financially dependent on another person right now. If you break up and that person moves out or kicks you out, you are not going to be prepared. By being responsible for your own life, you'll have a better education, a better sense of self, and more experience to bring to your marriage, whenever you choose it.

Resources

Book

Horowitz, S. (1995). *The penny-pinching hedonist: How to live like royalty with a peasant's pocketbook.* Northampton, MA: Accurate Writing & More.

Websites

Four-H Council
> http://www.fourhcouncil.edu/

Frugal Fun.com
> http://www.frugalfun.com

A Frugal, Simple Life
> http://hometown.aol.com/dsimple/

Volunteer Match
> http://www.volunteermatch.org/
> Find a volunteer opportunity that matches your interests.

Motor Vehicle Divisions

Here are websites and phone numbers to find our more information about vehicle registration and driver's licenses in every state.

Alabama
> http://www.dps.state.al.us/
> 334/242-4400

Alaska
> http://www.state.ak.us/local/akpages/
> ADMIN/dmv/
> 907/269-5551

Arizona
> http://www.dot.state.az.us/MVD/
> mvd.htm
> Phoenix 602/255-0072
> Tucson 520/629-9808
> Elsewhere: 1-800-251-5866

Arkansas
> http://www.state.ar.us/dfa/
> your_vehicle.html
> 1-888-389-8336

California
> http://www.dmv.ca.gov/
> 1-800-777-0133

Colorado
> http://www.mv.state.co.us/mv.html
> 303/205-5600

Connecticut
> http://www.ct.gov/dmv/site/default.asp
> Hartford: 860/263-5700
> Elsewhere: 1-800-842-8222

Delaware
> http://www.delaware.gov/yahoo/DMV
> Wilmington: 302/434-3200
> Dover: 302/744-2500
> New Castle: 302/326-5000
> Georgetown: 302/853-1000

District of Columbia
> http://www.dmv.washingtondc.gov/
> main.shtm
> 202/727-5000

Florida
> http://www.hsmv.state.fl.us/
> 850/922-9000

Georgia

http://www.dmvs.ga.gov/
678/413-8400

Hawaii

http://www.co.honolulu.hi.us/csd/
vehicle/index.htm
808/532-7700

Idaho

http://www.itd.idaho.gov/dmv/index.htm
208/334-8606

Illinois

http://www.sos.state.il.us/services/
services_motorists.html
1-800-252-8980

Indiana

http://www.state.in.us/bmv/
317/233-6000

Iowa

http://www.dot.state.ia.us/mvd/index.htm
1-800-532-1121

Kansas

http://www.accesskansas.org/living/
cars-transportation.html
785/296-3963

Kentucky

http://www.kytc.state.ky.us/
502/564-6800

Louisiana

http://omv.dps.state.la.us/
1-877-DMV-LINE

Maine

http://www.state.me.us/sos/bmv/
207/624-9000

Maryland

http://www.mva.state.md.us/
1-800-950-1682

Massachusetts

http://www.state.ma.us/rmv/
In the 339, 617, 781, or 857 area codes
or from out-of-state: 617/351-4500
In the 351, 413, 508, 774, or 978 area
codes: 1-800-858-3926

Michigan

http://www.michigan.gov/sos/0,1607,
7-127-1627---,00.html
517/322-1460

Minnesota

http://www.dps.state.mn.us/dvs/
index.html
651/296-6911

Mississippi

http://www.mmvc.state.ms.us/
601/987-3995

Missouri

http://www.dor.state.mo.us/
573/751-4600

Montana

http://www.doj.state.mt.us/driving
406/444-1773

Nebraska

http://www.dmv.state.ne.us//
index.htm
402/471-3861

Nevada

http://nevadadmv.state.nv.us/
Las Vegas: 702/486-4368
Reno/Sparks/Carson City:
775/684-4368
Rural Nevada or out-of-state:
1-877-368-7828

New Hampshire

http://www.state.nh.us/dmv/
index.html
603/271-2251

New Jersey

http://www.state.nj.us/mvs/
1-888-486-3339
Out-of-state: 609/292-6500

New Mexico

http://www.state.nm.us/tax/mvd/
mvd_home.htm
1-888-MVD-INFO

New York

http://www.nydmv.state.ny.us/

From area codes 212, 347, 646, 718, and 917: 212/645-5550

From area codes 516, 631, 845, and 914: 1-800-342-5368

From all other area codes in New York State: 1-800-225-5368

Out-of-state: 518/473-5595

North Carolina

http://www.dmv.dot.state.nc.us/driverlicense/

919/715-7000

North Dakota

http://www.state.nd.us/dot/

701/328-2581

Ohio

http://www.state.oh.us/odps/division/bmv/bmv.html

614/752-7500

Oklahoma

http://www.dps.state.ok.us/dls/

405/523-1571

Oregon

http://www.odot.state.or.us/dmv/DriverLicensing/licensing.htm

503/945-5000

Pennsylvania

http://www.dmv.state.pa.us/

1-800-932-4600

Out-of-state: 717/391-6190

Rhode Island

http://www.dmv.state.ri.us/

401/588-3020

South Carolina

http://www.scdps.org/dmv/

803/737-4000

South Dakota

http://www.state.sd.us/dcr/dl/sddriver.html

1-800-952-3696

Sioux Falls: 605/362-2746

Out-of-state 605/773-6883

Tennessee

http://www.state.tn.us/safety/nav2.html

615/741-3954

Texas

http://www.dot.state.tx.us/txdot.htm

512/416-4800

Utah

http://www.dmv.utah.com/

Salt Lake: 801/297-7780

Everywhere else: 1-800-DMV-UTAH

Vermont

http://www.aot.state.vt.us/dmv/dmvhp.htm

802/828-2000

Virginia

http://www.dmv.state.va.us/

1-866-368-5463

1-800-435-5137

Washington

http://www.dol.wa.gov/ds/dl.htm

360/902-3900

West Virginia

http://www.wvdot.com/6_motorists/dmv/6G_DMV.HTM

304/558-3900

1-800-642-9066

Wisconsin

http://www.dot.wisconsin.gov/drivers/

608/266-2353

Wyoming

http://dot.state.wy.us/web/driver_services/index.html

307/777-4800

Departments of Education

To ask questions about your state's education laws and programs, check out the map or the state-by-state listing at the U.S. Department of Education's website. You can click on your state on the map at http://www.ed.gov/Programs/EROD/ERODmap.html or in the list at http://www.ed.gov/Programs/EROD/statelist.html, and the site will give you a list of Internet links to your state's department of education and other local education-related resources.

Alabama
334/242-9950

Alaska
907/465-2800

Arizona
602/542-4361

Arkansas
501/682-4475

California
916/319-0791

Colorado
303/866-6600

Connecticut
860/713-6548

Delaware
302/739-4601

District of Columbia
202/724-4222

Florida
850/487-1785

Georgia
404/656-2800

Hawaii
808/586-3230

Idaho
208/332-6800

Illinois
217/782-4648

Indiana
317/232-0808

Iowa
515/281-5294

Kansas
785/296-3201

Kentucky
1-800-533-5372

Louisiana
1-877-453-2721

Maine
207/624-6705

Maryland
410/767-0100

Massachusetts
781/338-3000

Michigan
517/373-3324

Minnesota
651/582-8200

Mississippi
601/359-3513

Missouri
573/751-4212

Montana
1-888-231-9393

Nebraska
402/471-2295

Nevada
775/687-9200

New Hampshire
603/271-3494

New Jersey
609/292-4041

New Mexico
505/827-5800

New York
518/474-3852

North Carolina
919/807-3300

North Dakota
701/328-2260

Ohio
1-877-644-6338

Oklahoma
405/521-3301

Oregon
503/378-3569

Pennsylvania
717/783-6788

Rhode Island
401/222-4600

South Carolina
803/734-8815

South Dakota
605/773-3134

Tennessee
615/741-2731

Texas
512/463-9734

Utah
801/538-7500

Vermont
802/828-3154

Virginia
1-800-292-3820

Washington
360/725-6000

West Virginia
304/558-2546

Wisconsin
1-800-441-4563

Wyoming
307/777-7675

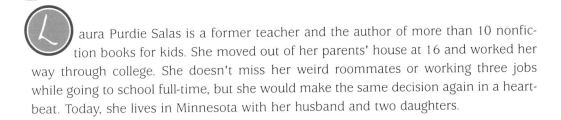

Laura Purdie Salas is a former teacher and the author of more than 10 nonfiction books for kids. She moved out of her parents' house at 16 and worked her way through college. She doesn't miss her weird roommates or working three jobs while going to school full-time, but she would make the same decision again in a heartbeat. Today, she lives in Minnesota with her husband and two daughters.